## Additional Praise for *Timeless Leadership*

"Timeless Leadership *is an invaluable contribution to the literature on leadership. In his inimitable style and with an extraordinary gift for compelling metaphors, Debashis Chatterjee brings the eternal truths of the* Bhagavad Gita *to fresh and vibrant life, ready to be absorbed and applied by leaders of all types of organizations. Prof. Chatterjee has arrived at the 'simplicity on the other side of complexity,' the mark of true mastery of his subject. This book is a treasure, a must read for any one aspiring to be a conscious business leader and a fully realized human being.*"

—Rajendra Sisodia, Professor of Marketing,
Bentley University

"*What can ancient Indian mythology teach today's global leaders? A great deal, according to this engaging analysis by Debashis Chatterjee, who considers leadership through the lens of the* Bhagavad Gita. *Readers will benefit from Chatterjee's close reading of the* Gita, *as he traces the leadership journey of a classic hero, Arjuna. We learn that leaders reach their full potential only if they overcome the limitations of their ego. They do this by cultivating a mentality that sees reality clearly, not through the faulty perceptions of a mind unsettled by a 'mob' of emotion and conditioned impulses. Chatterjee's leader is courageous but also humbled by the quest for profound self-knowledge that leads to truth and the ability to work with the devotion of 'love made visible.' Anyone seeking clarity about leadership's ultimate foundation will embrace this book.*"

—Dipak C. Jain, Dean, INSEAD

# TIMELESS
# LEADERSHIP

# TIMELESS LEADERSHIP

## *18 Leadership Sutras from* The Bhagavad Gita

### DEBASHIS CHATTERJEE

John Wiley & Sons Singapore Pte. Ltd.

Copyright © 2012 John Wiley & Sons Singapore Pte. Ltd.

Published in 2012 by John Wiley & Sons Singapore Pte. Ltd., 1 Fusionopolis Walk, #07-01, Solaris South Tower, Singapore 138628

**Other Wiley Editorial Offices**

John Wiley & Sons, 111 River Street, Hoboken, NJ 07030, USA

John Wiley & Sons, The Atrium, Southern Gate, Chichester, West Sussex, P019 8SQ, United Kingdom

John Wiley & Sons (Canada) Ltd., 5353 Dundas Street West, Suite 400, Toronto, Ontario, M9B 6HB, Canada

John Wiley & Sons (Australia) Ltd., 42 McDougall Street, Milton, Queensland 4064, Australia

Wiley-VCH, Boschstrasse 12, D-69469 Weinheim, Germany

ISBN 978-0-470-82427-6 (cloth)
ISBN 978-0-470-82925-7 (ePDF)
ISBN 978-0-470-82924-0 (Mobi)
ISBN 978-0-470-82926-4 (ePub)

Typeset in 11/13 pt. BemboStd by MPS Limited, Chennai, India.
Printed in Singapore by Markono Print Media.

10 9 8 7 6 5 4 3 2 1

*This work is dedicated to Narayandas Chatterjee,*
*who now resides in the timeless.*

# CONTENTS

## SUTRA 3    Karma Yoga
*Leaders Enter the Timeless Cycle of Action*                    **33**

## SUTRA 4    Timeless Leaders Pursue
##              Purpose as the Source of
##              Supreme Power                                  **47**

## SUTRA 5    Leadership Is the Art of Undoing
*The State of Detached Engagement*                             **59**

# A NOTE ABOUT THE TEXT

The *Bhagavad Gita* is a timeless text of about 700 verses. It is a spiritual classic that originated in India many years before Christ was born. The book appeared as an episode in the battle of Kurukshetra in Northern India. The *Bhagavad Gita* takes the form of a conversation between Krishna and Arjuna. The themes of the conversation range from the vast Cosmos to the inner-most soul of a human being, often referred to as the Self.

*Timeless Leadership* weaves this battlefield conversation into a narrative on the problems faced by leaders such as Arjuna and the solution provided by Krishna from a perspective that is both compelling and contemporary. This conversation between Arjuna and Krishna is narrated by Sanjaya to the blind king Dhritarashtra, who is eager to know the outcome of the battle; thus the book is a narrative within a narrative.

The Dean of the Harvard Business School, Professor Nitin Nohria, in an informal conversation, described to me the relevance and message of the *Gita* in a way that cleared any doubt I had about the contemporary relevance of this text. He said, "What Emerson is to America and Confucius is to China, Krishna is to India." I have known several Indian CEOs who have made it to the Fortune 100 list to echo the same feeling about Krishna's teachings to Arjuna. I trust this work is relevant for leaders around the world. I hope Krishna inspires leaders of all kinds to lead in their world in a way that makes the world a happier and a safer place for new generations.

This book is the result of a decade-long attempt to *trans-create* rather than translate the *Gita* for insights in leadership. The *Gita*'s unrivalled status as a spiritual classic rendered in Sanskrit made this trans-creation a formidable task. A literal translation of the ancient text would create insurmountable roadblocks for today's readers. I have read through more than 200 interpretations of the *Gita*, ranging from people well-known in the western world, such as Gandhi, Emerson, and Thoreau, to revered authors from the Indian tradition, such as Swami Vivekananda, founder of the Ramakrishna Mission, and Swami Chinmayananda, founder of the Chinmaya Mission, and a wide variety of more contemporary authors.

From my research I have presented 18 sutras from the *Gita*. Each sutra serves as a cognitive unit or a chapter title that compresses the message of the whole chapter. The word *sutra* literally means a thread (as in a thread that weaves the beads of a necklace together) that combines different sub-themes of a chapter as a unified whole. In well-known Indian texts such as the *Yoga Sutra* of Patanjali or Vatsayana's *Kama Sutra*, the word *sutra* denotes a short aphoristic statement that holds the attention of the reader or listener to the essence of the text's message. In Buddhist texts, the oral teachings of the Buddha were recorded in the form of sutras. This served as a device for the reader to memorize the text with greater ease.

The Sanskrit word *sukta*, which means "well spoken" or "good news," according to some scholars has the same meaning conveyed by the word *sutra*. This has the same import as the word *Gospel*, which refers to Christ's teachings. I have done the best I could to present the good news that Krishna delivers to Arjuna in the midst of the battlefield. I have taken the liberty to recreate the message of the *Gita* so as to make it more communicative to contemporary audiences around the world. In this, I believe, I have been able to glean 18 key messages of the *Gita* without diluting the core of its status as a sacred text. In short, I have not traded reverence for relevance.

The 18 sutras of the *Bhagavad Gita* have deep philosophical as well as practical implications for leaders of the third millennium. In this book, Krishna literally guides Arjuna and indeed all leaders like Arjuna through the ABCs of leadership. Here, *A* represents *Authenticity* or truth, which is the core value of leaders; *B* stands for *Being*, which is the raw material for becoming a leader; and *C* stands for *Convergence*, which a leader achieves between his current reality and his goal, or between a problem and its solution. Indeed, as a text, the *Bhagavad Gita* does not separate the problem from the solution. Arjuna, a leader-in-the-making, discovers the breakthrough solution to life's most persistent problems in the midst of the battlefield. Corporate warriors and leaders who see themselves in this millennial march of evolution of humankind and human-centered organizations may find the message of the *Gita* truly life-changing.

*Timeless Leadership* will have served its purpose if the readers of this book find something of relevance to their life and work that is for them both timeless and timely.

# ACKNOWLEDGMENTS

This work is the outcome of diligent study and conversations on the *Bhagavad Gita* with many masters for over 10 years. It is impossible for anyone to read or write on the *Gita* without living some of it. The *Gita* is a timeless manual for the art of living. My father, Narayandas Chatterjee, was making some personal notes on his understanding of the *Gita* when he passed away in September 2009. It was a timeless aspiration that he nurtured in his heart and that even his death could not interrupt. Therefore, I lovingly dedicate this work to the son of my grandfather, Jatindramohan Chatterjee.

I wish to acknowledge my debt of gratitude to C.J. Hwu, Nick Melchior, and my editor, Emilie Herman, of Wiley, for their extraordinary patience in waiting for the manuscript, and to Professor Ted Malloch of Yale University, world-renowned author Professor Jagdish Sheth, Professor Raj Sisodia, Mr. N.R. Narayanamurthy of Infosys—for their encouraging comments. My heartfelt thanks to Mr. Nitish Jain for sending me on a paid sabbatical visit to Rishikesh to study with the ancient gurus who lived the *Gita*. I remember with love the contribution made by G Narayana, who initiated me into those austerities of life that helped me understand the *Gita* more than all the hundred-odd commentaries I read on the sacred text. I acknowledge my debt to my friend for many years, Prasad Kaipa, for finding a new interpretation for the acronym *GPS* in the mental and spiritual context; to Dr. Srikumar Rao, internationally known author and friend, for painstakingly reading the manuscript as well as introducing the notion of alternative reality into my mindspace. Special thanks to my executive assistant Mr. Sojan George and my research assistant Ramya, and to my colleagues and students in IIM, Kozhikode, for allowing me precious time off from my role as director of this great institution to find time for this book. Many of the ideas in the *Gita* have shaped my thoughts and our collective vision for the Institute.

My gratitude is also due to Swami Tejomayananda and Acharya Soumendranath for sharing their beings with me. To those countless sages and saints of India and the larger world, on whose lives and wisdom I have based my understanding of Krishna's message to Arjuna, I bow my head in love and reverence.

As for Aditi, Shrishti, and Siddharth—extensions of my life—you will share more of my heart and mind now that the writing of this book is finally over.

# INTRODUCTION

# THE CONTEXT
# OF THE *GITA*

Suspended in the middle of a battle, Arjuna, the leader-warrior, refuses to fight. The epic battle between the Kauravas and the Pandavas comes to a standstill.

The *Bhagavad Gita* zooms in on many moments of truth with an imminent battle in the backdrop: the fierce blowing of conch shells like lions roaring; massive movements of soldiers; neighing horses; battle banners fluttering on both sides. Arjuna, the greatest warrior of his time, is driven in a magnificent chariot by his friend, mentor, and divine guide, Krishna. Arjuna is leading the battle on behalf of the Pandavas, who have lost their kingdom to their own kin, the Kauravas. In a wicked plot, the Kauravas have unjustly dethroned the Pandavas. This is a battle for a just cause—a battle of redemption. Arjuna says to Krishna: "Let me have a look at my enemies before I fight them." Krishna drives the glittering chariot, pulled by four white horses, right into midfield between the two warring camps. Arjuna eyes his enemies: his former friends, his great teachers, and his revered uncles. He is in deep sorrow. He wonders before Krishna how he can kill his own people, who are supposed to be loved and respected. Wouldn't a battle lead to the destruction of society? Wouldn't that lead to the breakdown of established institutions of caste and tribe? Wouldn't this war lead to the disintegration of family and ancestral virtues? Arjuna slumps down in his chariot in anguished indecision. His hands begin to shake and he lays down his bow and arrow. In a dramatic turn of events, Arjuna seems completely lost in despair. He urges Krishna to show him the way.

# THE WARRIOR'S JOURNEY

## Leaders Embrace Discontinuity and Death

Death is very likely the single best invention of Life. It is Life's change agent. It clears out the old to make way for the new. Right now the new is you, but someday not too long from now, you will gradually become the old and be cleared away. Sorry to be so dramatic, but it is quite true.

—Steve Jobs in his Stanford Graduation Speech, Spring 2005

Leading an organization of the twenty-first century requires more than just a firefighter's skill of putting out fires as and when they reach alarming proportions. A firefighter is trained to fight and deal with urgency. However, a leader of the future will have to negotiate not only the urgent but also the emergent—that which is not yet obvious, like a raging fire, but will emerge in the future. A leader of a major organization remarked that sometimes he does not have the luxury of choosing his battles; he has to fight each battle as it emerges from the environment and presents itself. The unpredictability of the battle for market share and mindshare, the volatility of the environment, and the rapid-fire changes that are happening in the business and political landscape have all the trappings of a full-scale war. A mere firefighter cannot pretend to be a warrior. The ability to deal with the emergent conditions of the war demands much more than functional skills. It requires a rare leadership virtue called *awareness*. The journey of awareness starts with Self-awareness. Krishna leads Arjuna on this journey.

The leader at work is a fighter who wants to be a warrior. To qualify as a warrior the fighter first needs to attend to his unfinished business: the fight within himself. The archer has to first arrest his own mind before he can aim for the bull's-eye. A leader of an organization who wants to achieve a target has to first focus on his inner resolve to do so. The fighter Arjuna's battleground is his own self. There are a million mutinies going on inside the self: the fight between reason and emotion; between the head and the heart; between what one is and what one can be. In contrast, Krishna the warrior has finished the fight with himself. The true warrior does not deplete his energy in emotional drama that binds him to self-defeating patterns of fear and guilt. He pierces through his self-created enemies with the sword of Self-awareness and the shield of sharp discrimination.

Arjuna represents the quest of the warrior in all of us. This is a quest that seeks answers to life's most persistent riddles: Who am I? Why am I doing battle with this life? A quest can start with no more than a question. Arjuna is the question. His mentor, Krishna, is the answer. Arjuna is still a fighter. Krishna is the consummate warrior. He holds sway as the lord of his own mind. In this way, it is very crucial for an organizational leader to achieve mastery over his own mind before he can influence the minds of others.

Krishna is timeless wisdom in human form; he is wholeness embodied. He is the unity of life in diversity of forms. He integrates the divisive aspects of our war-torn self into one whole understanding of who we really are. In this understanding our separate and conflicting ego-edges dissolve. We find connection even with our sworn enemies in the unity of purpose: our collective sacred identity—the *dharma* of our soul. Krishna teaches Arjuna how to lead in the battle of life with his undying and imperishable soul Self. He teaches us the secret of invincibility.

## ALL WARS ARE FIRST FOUGHT IN THE MIND

Arjuna said,

> My mind is in a whirl seeing my own kin facing death in my hands.
>> My mouth is dry with fear.
>> All my limbs are shaking. My bow keeps slipping through my hand.
>> My skin burns, my brain reels, I am unable to stand.
>
> *(1.29–30)*

All wars are first fought in the mind. Therefore, it is in the mind that all wars must first be won. Arjuna, the great warrior, has a mental breakdown in the middle of the battlefield. He does not wish to kill his kinsmen. In his refusal to take up arms against his near-and-dear ones, Arjuna heightens the battle that goes on within our own minds. The near-and-dear ones are often those thoughts and emotions we are deeply attached to. The people we are closest to are the ones we very often think of or feel strongly about. Kinship is determined by familiarity in thought and emotion. Whomever we are most familiar with becomes our "family." For the leader of an organization the conventions of business as usual have to be challenged. These must be first challenged within one's immediate environment or one's own family.

The war of the *Bhagavad Gita* is happening within the family. Arjuna, representing the Pandavas, and Duryodhona, representing the Kauravas, are cousins. Arjuna has been robbed and deprived of what is due to him and is poised to fight Duryodhona for the kingdom that is rightfully his. Arjuna's dilemma is that he is emotionally attached to his family, whom he must now fight for a just cause. But the real war is inside Arjuna's mind: a mind that is struggling to wriggle out of familiar feelings and emotions. This war is a battle to break out of mental moulds. It is Arjuna's struggle to evolve out of the cocoon of his comfort zone.

Arjuna is an unfinished leader. He is a work in progress. His evolving life takes him through conflict of choice. The human mind evolves through choices. Arjuna's choice is between fighting and shying away from the fight. Only the human condition presents such choices. Animals don't have to make such choices. The animal instinctively fights or flees. The tiger does not ask whether it should kill its prey or shy away from it. The buffalo does not make the choice to step aside on a busy street and politely allow its herd to pass by. The tiger is bound by its instinct to chase and kill its prey when it is hungry. The buffalo is bound by its instinct to move in a huddle with its herd. But the leader of an organization has to overcome the *herd instinct* that gets in the way of progress.

Thus the human condition comes with a boon and a curse: We have the boon of choosing and the curse of the conflicts that we must face when we have many choices. Whenever there is conflict in the world, human beings have to realize that there is no such thing as a conflict in reality. All conflicts reside in the content of our own mind. The summer has no conflict with the winter. Only the mind that gets conditioned by the warmth of summer resists the winter. The leader within an organization has to be deeply Self-aware to see that all conflicts start in the mind-space.

Conflict arises when a mind is reluctant to get out of its entrenchment in a familiar way of life. Arjuna's mind is wedded to an established order. Whenever that order is threatened, the human mind enters into conflict with itself. His mind recoils from the breakdown of that established order in the event of a war. Arjuna is a struggling fighter. He is unable to step out of the prison of his own mind in which he is fighting himself.

## THE MIND IS A MOB

The agitated mind is a mob of thoughts and emotions. At any point in time thoughts swarm across the mental space like bustling crowds in a metropolis. Arjuna is dejected and despondent. He is unable to focus his thoughts on a single point of action. He is unable to lift his bow and arrow and get on with the war.

What happens when the mind behaves like an unruly mob? It loses its power to act wisely. When the mind is unruly and indecisive, the body follows through non-action. Like a manager unable to make a stressful decision, Arjuna creates an alibi of hollow words to defend his crippled will. He says he would rather be killed than kill his own kinsmen. He forgets that he is in a righteous war against the Kauravas, who have unjustly usurped his kingdom. He offers weak arguments to defend his decision to flee the war. His personal ego and emotions overshadow his powers of discrimination.

When the mind behaves like a mob there are countless mutinies going on within it. Inside Arjuna's mind the battle rages between forgiveness and anger, between valour and cowardice, between faith and doubt, and between happiness and grief. In a war-torn mind, the will to act ceases to function. Will is the energy source of all our action. When a leader confronts turbulence in an organization his will to take decisive action is seriously impaired by an irresolute mind.

The energy of our will has to be freed from the confusions and conflicts of the mind. Arjuna cannot free his will from the network of reactions that arises in his mind as he contemplates the prospects of war. The flow of will is possible only when the mind is free from the throes of reaction. A leader whose will is crippled wonders, "What will people think about me in my organization if I act this way instead of that?" He becomes a victim of self-doubt. His fragmented mind functions like the surface waves of a stormy ocean. Such a mind is unable to reflect the depths of the still ocean. The mind in conflict is like those raging waves that obscure the will that lies buried in the depths of our psyche.

Arjuna has been preparing for this righteous war for many years. He is a born warrior, yet he is still stuck in the fight with himself. Arjuna has fragmented his whole life into parts just as separate waves fragment the ocean into multiple aspects. As he is stricken by grief he is merely repeating patterns. Grief-stricken, Arjuna is fruitlessly lamenting like the weakened waves of the sea breaking on a rocky shore. Arjuna's choice is not about violence or nonviolence; it is about fragmentation versus wholeness. When the mind is fragmented, our perception of life gets distorted just as the multiple waves distort the unity of the ocean.

Let's go back to the psychology of the mob to understand Arjuna's mind. A mob is an unruly and capricious crowd. In a mob the individual loses the power to think deeply and act out the individual will. A mob is unsteady and its actions are no longer governed by rationality or a steady flow of individual will. When we are fragmented, as Arjuna is, our brain is unsteady and the nervous system is tensed. Our emotional composure is thrown out of balance.

Our experience is like that of a man who is drowning in a storm-tossed sea. How do we react under such circumstances? We just grasp at any straw to save our lives. This is exactly what Arjuna is doing. This is what most leaders do when they are caught in crisis within an organization. They express their own inadequacy through worry, impulsive behavior, and unsteady will. They hold onto their own restless minds like a drowning man holding onto a straw. Think of those leaders who were heading those financial institutions that were torn apart in crisis. Or, think of those autocratic rulers in Egypt and the Middle East who were barely hanging onto their thrones in utter desperation!

Krishna is about to teach Arjuna the way to deal with the problem he faces. Krishna is a warrior and he has already resolved the fight in his own mind. He is about to convince Arjuna that he is behaving like a mob because he has identified himself with his restless mind. Krishna teaches Arjuna the art of rising above the turbulence of the mind. A fighter like Arjuna gets caught in this turbulence. A warrior like Krishna observes any potential turbulence or disorder in the mind and brings it to order. Krishna would urge Arjuna to know the disorder of his own mind by observing it. Therefore, Krishna would urge Arjuna to look at his own mind and know it. You can't look at something or know something unless you are separate from the phenomenon that you are looking at or wish to know. You can't look at your own eyes when you are looking through them. Likewise, you can't know the taste of your own tongue, can you? You have to be separate from the phenomenon that you wish to see or know before you can truly know it. You can take a photograph or a look at a mirror-image of your own eyes in order to see them as a separate entity. Krishna will clarify to Arjuna that his restless mind must be the *object* of his knowledge. To lead any organization, objectivity in dealing with one's own mind is a crucial virtue. Leaders can acquire this objectivity only when they know how to bypass their ego when they are dealing with their own mind.

## THE EGO IS A DISPOSABLE IDEA

Arjuna will need to distance and detach himself from his own ego, which is preventing him from knowing his own mind. The ego is like a disposable idea. An idea is like mental tissue paper that must be disposed of when it outlives its utility. Yet we hang on to ideas as though they were inseparable from us. For a long time in human history most people held onto the idea that the Earth was the center of the universe and that every other planetary body, including the Sun, was moving around the Earth. When Nicolaus Copernicus formulated enough scientific evidence of a Sun-centered universe, the Earth was displaced from its assumed center.

Arjuna is hanging onto his ego, which is nothing more than the illusory center of his universe. From this ego-center he sees others—his own kith and kin—through the emotional filters of despair and despondency. Arjuna is obsessed merely with the idea of death. His mentor, Krishna, is like a spiritual Copernicus. He sets out to displace Arjuna's ego from the center of his identity and makes him see a different world with the help of subtler discrimination. In this different world, it is not the *ego* but the *soul Self* that is the central organizing principle of his universe. Krishna urges: "Mortality, Arjuna, is nothing but your idea of death because the soul Self never dies—it only changes costumes as it takes up and discards bodies. Your suffering is based on nothing but a disposable idea: the misplaced notion that you are your body-mind rather than your soul Self."

Arjuna speaks from the center of his ego as he grieves for his own relatives, whom he is poised to take on in the battlefield. He feels that to kill his people, even if this was a righteous war, would be to stain his life with unhappiness and misery. Krishna speaks from the soul-center as he counsels Arjuna: The wise grieve neither for the dead nor for the living form. Krishna argues that grief is the ego's attachment to a *form* of life. Life is like an ocean and life-forms are the waves rising from the ocean. The ocean is the enduring reality—the waves have no independent existence without the ocean. The waves simply rise only to fall. He makes Arjuna realize that the rise and fall of his enemies are like the rise and fall of waves. From the soul's perspective, life is timeless and life-forms are temporary. So why grieve for life-forms when life itself never ceases to be. Life-forms are like those disposable ideas that play on interminable life just as waveforms play on the inexhaustible ocean.

Have you ever thought of war as a clash of ideas and ideals? Very often that's how most wars begin. When old ideas are sought to be replaced by new ideas, war becomes inevitable. We have seen the war of communism versus capitalism or the war of science and religion. Our old ways of thinking and feeling are like our relatives. However, we are constrained to fight them whenever we need to switch to different ways of looking at the world.

Arjuna, not unlike today's corporate warriors, is attached to old ideas. He is in a comfort zone of familiar ideas about his identity and his relationship with others. Krishna, his wise charioteer, brings him out of the comfort zone to do battle with his own near-and-dear ones as well as his outworn ideas. This war is truly an adventure of ideas.

It is also about transformation: a change of mind and heart.

Very often the transformation of leaders happens during a crisis. Arjuna is in the middle of a mental crisis. He has a nervous breakdown seeing all of his brothers, cousins, uncles, and grandsons arrayed against him. All the symptoms of this crisis are evident in his body: His mouth is dry, his limbs are paralyzed by inaction, and he is trembling with fear. To defend himself against fear, Arjuna has taken up the alibi of nonviolence. Arjuna's ego has taken over as the narrator of the script of nonviolence crafted by his fickle mind. The ego cannot deal with threats to its own continuity; it cannot embrace discontinuity in its habitual storyline. Arjuna's storyline is about preservation of tradition and life through nonviolence. But how can the nonviolence of a fearful mind amount to anything? How can such nonviolence deal with the assault of a battle-hungry opposition? Krishna lifts Arjuna from a mere idea of nonviolence based on a false appraisal to another standpoint of perception. He points out to Arjuna the need to look beyond the discontinuity of life-forms to the larger continuity of timeless *dharma*—the law of life.

## LEADERS EMBRACE DISCONTINUITY BY DISPOSSESSING THE EGO

To look beyond the ego is to embrace discontinuity. One head of state once said, "It's amazing how many people beat you at golf now that you're no longer President." Life moves on discontinuously; the ego struggles to hold back. Life is multidimensional. Ego is personality centered and one-dimensional. Life is timeless and free-flowing. The ego is conditioned by time, space, and personality.

Krishna leads Arjuna to evolve on the path of timeless wisdom. He teaches his young, crestfallen protégé how to embrace the discontinuity of all relationships with the universe that are material in nature. He says: "Arjuna, your soul Self experiences through this material body the passing spectacle of infancy, youth, and old age. After death the soul discontinues its attachment with the body and passes on to another one." It is like seeing slow-motion slides of a flower blooming and withering away before we move on to the next slide. So he urges Arjuna to observe how material bodies that experience heat and cold, pain and happiness are themselves temporary locations of the imperishable soul. The wise person is the one who does not grieve for finite and fleeting forms. A leader who is established in this wisdom is sustained by the timeless order of life.

By embracing discontinuity leaders reinvent the future. The future is often discontinuous with the past. Past forms perish; old relationships fade away. Life continuously renews itself through the birth of new forms. An old leaf trembling on a tree is soon replaced by a new one waiting to take its place. In the physical universe of nature we see a ceaseless death so that new life-forms can be born.

A timeless leader practices the art of voluntary elimination. He knows what activities—physical or mental—must be given up so that an organization becomes more productive. A new organization is born in the womb of the old organization. A new generation of new recruits is forever striving to replace an old generation of employees. It is a war of sorts: a clash of perspectives and worldviews. This kind of war is inevitable. We cannot shy away from it.

Nations have evolved through war. War is the price they have paid to buy peace. But wars have awakened the hidden energies and potential of people in many parts of the world. They have actually made the quest for peace and stability much more intense in these nations. Organizations are no different. In order to sustain in the long run, they have to wage a war against deadwood thinking and decaying organizational practices. Old habits die hard. A leader has to destabilise existing forms of thought and action. A leader has to learn to deal with discontinuity.

Discontinuity comes with an obvious sense of loss. How do leaders deal with it? They do so by embracing the deeper continuity of the spirit underlying the fragmentation of forms. This is done through the power of internalization of one's energies. Habitually, our sensory energies go out into the world. Our eyes open outward; the skin senses the outer environment through its tactility. The senses register a world of endless variety and differentiation while looking outward. While looking inward, the leader is able to retrace the energy from the diversifying sensory apparatus to the unity of soul within. His outgoing, differentiating, and fragmenting tendencies are balanced by his internalizing and integrating and meditative mind. It is here that he experiences continuity of the one conscious soul Self in the apparent discontinuity of sense-based data.

## THE SECRET OF INVINCIBILITY: THE CONQUEST OF THE BINARY MIND

Krishna says to Arjuna, "The leader whose soul is unmoved by circumstances and who accepts pleasure and pain with equanimity is invincible." The mind of the fighter swings between the fear of losing and the allure of winning. This is the law of the binary mind. Such a mind cannot see beyond the duality of conflicting emotions.

The real duty of the warrior is not just to fight a righteous war. The warrior's aspiration is to enhance his own evolutionary capacity while he is involved in the fight. He needs to engage his entire physical and mental energy while fighting. To keep his mind steady in the fight, he needs to stop wasting the energy that his conflicting mind consumes. He needs to overcome his emotional turmoil rather than be overwhelmed by it.

The first secret of invincibility is to conquer the binary mind that flutters at the slightest provocation. This mind leads the fighter to an either/or universe. You either win or you lose. You either kill or you get killed. This is how the reptilian fight-or-flight brain works: You either eat or are eaten by your foe.

When the fighter evolves as a warrior his discriminating intellect has awakened. With the help of this intellect he is able to detect that the real battle is going on inside his binary mind. He watches dispassionately the False Evidence shown As Real (FEAR) with a mind that is not focused on the field of the battle. With the awakening of this discriminating intellect, the warrior refocuses his entire mental energy in the battle itself. He knows that he cannot always determine whether he will win or lose—that will depend on multiple factors over which he may or may not have control. However, he can decide to go to battle with utmost intensity. He will not die in his mind many times before his death. This will make him invincible.

Why is he invincible? A mind that harbors dejection loses the battle even before it is fought. Arjuna is in such a state. His intellect is unable to engage his mind in the ensuing battle. When the mind wavers it is at work against itself. The binary mind fluctuates between resoluteness and irresoluteness. Such is the mind of a fighter who is consumed by the fight that rages within him. In contrast, the warrior is able to see through the futility of this fight with the help of his discerning intellect. The warrior becomes invincible when his work and his goal become one. As two eyes become one sight and many stars become one light, the divided mind of the fighter becomes one in the warrior. He achieves invincibility by conquering his binary mind.

## SELF IS THE CAUSE; SELF IS THE EFFECT

A loser is self-made, and so is a winner. The raw material for all our actions and all our achievements comes from our Self. As a great mountaineer would say, "It is not the mountains we conquer but ourselves."

In the ultimate analysis, leadership is Self-situated: You are the cause and you are also the effect. Think of a stressful problem you are facing at home or in the office. An investment banker tells us: "I have a huge workload problem." We enquire, "Yes, we understand there is a lot of work for you out there. But, where is the load? Can you show us where the load is? You aren't carrying a ton of bricks on your head as far as we can see." The banker thinks about that. The "load" is felt, not as a physical sensation, but as a *perception* in the mind. The mind is tied up in a perceptual knot. This knot is *not* a physical one, but rather a knot in perception.

Like Arjuna, the investment banker feels the knot of depression. But who has created the depression related to his "workload problem"? Obviously, the banker himself! He does this by the way he perceives the problem. He feels like Arjuna does: that the world will probably collapse around him if his problem isn't solved. So Arjuna's workload problem is one of faulty perception. Without getting rid of his faulty perception, Arjuna will be unable to get out from under the burden of the workload.

A veteran ironsmith burdened by a huge workload hired a novice who was willing to share his workload at very nominal pay.

The master smith began to instruct the young apprentice on the skill of hitting a piece of iron on anvil with a hammer. He told the apprentice:

"When I take the hot iron out of the fire, I will put it on the anvil; and then when the time is right I will nod my head. Right then you hit with all your might with the hammer."

The novice followed what he had perceived as the instruction: he hit the master's head with the hammer!

Clearly, the master was a victim of his apprentice's self-created perception. The instruction was to hit the iron, but he hit the master's head instead. Arjuna is supposed to take up his bow and arrow and direct it toward the work at hand. Instead, his attention is diverted from the real work to the wasteful mental load that he carries.

The fighter perceives the knots in his perception as the problems of the world. Fighters see themselves poised before a self-created problem like a man who is ready to fight his own shadow. In truth, no one can win a fight with his own shadow. The only way to solve this problem of shadow-fighting is to be aware. It is through the light of awareness and not through physical or mental effort that the most persistent problems of the world are solved. Krishna is the light of awareness that takes Arjuna through the self-created shadows of doubt, dejection, and uncertainty. Krishna will accomplish this through a gradual shift in Arjuna's identity from a fighter of shadows to a warrior of light.

## HUNTING FOR THE *I*

Arjuna thinks that his problem is to get out of a depressing situation where he is a reluctant fighter. Krishna knows that the root of the problem is that Arjuna is hunting for his real identity. The warrior's primary hunt is for the *I* that is whole and all-embracing. It is the ultimate quest in all forms of human conflict. The human identity is fragmented in many ways: us-versus-them; me-versus-you; intellect-versus-emotion; old-versus-new; right-versus-wrong. War is merely a symptom that we are attempting to heal this disintegration. To heal is to find our "wholesome" identity in the journey.

Arjuna's problem is that he is focused on a microscopic *i*: his own ego wrapped in skin, bone, flesh, and blood. Krishna's solution is to take Arjuna to the macroscopic *I*: his soul Self that integrates him with his larger human identity. The microscopic *i* binds one body with another in a material relationship. This small *i* creates multiple divisions between one *i* and another. It functions through fragmentation of a larger human identity that is based on unity and its supporting values. However, the macroscopic *I* is the holder and beholder of these supporting values, such as truth, love, and freedom. This *I* is the source of timeless *dharma*: that which holds everything together.

Arjuna's kinsmen have violated *dharma* by their wrong actions. Therefore, they are bound by the law of the macroscopic universe to bear the consequences of their own actions. Arjuna is perplexed because he is emotionally attached to the small *i*. He is worried by the severance of his material and physical connection with his dear ones. Krishna puts Arjuna into the right hunt: the hunt for the larger *I* that he knows will resolve Arjuna's disintegration and set him on the path to victory. Krishna is not only Arjuna's charioteer; he is also a friend of Arjuna. But Krishna is more than that. He is the very essence of Arjuna's identity—Arjuna's real Soul Self:

> The fighter knocked at the door of his friend, the warrior.
>
> "Who is knocking?" asked the warrior from within.
>
> "It is i," replied the fighter.
>
> "Go back. This house is too small to hold both you and me," came the response from inside.
>
> The fighter withdrew and reflected for a long time on what the warrior had said.
>
> After many years he returned and knocked on the door again.
>
> "Who is knocking?," the voice from inside asked again.
>
> "It is you," said the fighter, who had now identified with the essence of the warrior.
>
> The door was flung open for the fighter to go inside the house.

The door of a new perception was opened when the small "i" of the fighter got integrated with the large "I" of the warrior.

# SUTRA 2

# INVINCIBLE WISDOM

## Leaders Create Alternative Reality

Arjuna's despondency deepens. His intellect is dulled by self-pity. Arjuna's mind is clouded by a reality that he constructs out of his emotionally turbulent mind. Krishna realizes that the only way to liberate Arjuna from his cowardice is to present to him an alternative reality. This is what timeless leaders do: They reframe reality in a way that gives hope to their followers, often in the most hopeless of circumstances. Krishna creates an alternative reality for Arjuna by showing him how to think like a victor rather than a victim. Krishna rouses Arjuna as he says, "How unbecoming of a hero is it to abandon a just war that was decided on after great deliberation? How can you protect your reputation if you retreat from the battle now?" His mentor's words begin to have an effect on Arjuna. The cloud of despair that had gathered around his mind has begun to disperse. The warrior in Arjuna has begun to stir from deep inertia. The alternative reality that Krishna creates for him begins to move Arjuna toward action. It is here that Krishna unfolds before Arjuna the path of invincible wisdom.

## GRIEF, PITY, AND SHAME: THE MIND'S GPS SYSTEM

Arjuna says to Krishna:

> My heart is overpowered by grief, pity, and shame;
> My mind is confused about whether to fight or to give in.
> Tell me decisively what I should do.
> I am your disciple. Instruct me for I have taken refuge in you.
>
> *(2.7)*

Arjuna's thoughts are guided by his mind's "GPS" system: *grief, pity*, and *shame*. The ordinary mind is a composition of thoughts plus feelings. Thoughts are like brick and feelings are like cement. Together they create the illusion of a concrete structure of reality. This concrete structure can be described as a *mental model*. When a mental model is guided by those shifting moods of grief, pity, and shame the world looks like a hopeless place.

Arjuna is not unlike a leader who has to navigate the corporate world through shifting moods that cloud his vision and distort his awareness. Fear of the boss, pressure of deadlines, grief over job losses, long hours of separation from family, self-pity and shame resulting from underperformance—all of these paralyze a person at work.

Here Krishna plays the role of the mentor. He urges Arjuna to examine his mental model. He almost mocks Arjuna as he says:

> You grieve for those who should not be grieved for;
> Yet you speak words of wisdom.
> The wise grieve neither for the living nor for the dead.
>
> *(2.12)*

Arjuna is overwhelmed by a sense of self-pity as he is unable to reconcile the fact of taking up arms against his dear ones even as he is attached to them. Krishna explains to Arjuna that his compassion is misplaced as such an attachment is illusory. Attachment to a rush of sensory stimulus from the world outside is causing waves of grief, pity, and shame in Arjuna. The sensory organs of Arjuna are like wild horses that he is struggling to hold back with the reins of his mind. These waves of emotional upheaval accompanied by negative mental chatter are causing havoc and preventing Arjuna from taking decisive action.

Krishna, Arjuna's charioteer and divine guide, teaches him how the wise follow the path of discrimination. He says:

> Look, Arjuna! Every physical body comes from worldly elements
> And returns again to these elements at death. So why should you lament?
> Souls cannot be slain, Arjuna, by any man or thing.
> Why do you grieve then over a living being?
>
> *(2.27)*

Krishna has clarity of vision that Arjuna lacks because the latter's perception is muddied by his faulty GPS system. Krishna rightly says that the physical body is a temporary compound of five elements and sooner or later the elements in the body will disintegrate at the end of a person's life. So what is the point of grieving over something that is impermanent?

Timeless leaders learn to discriminate between the real and the unreal. Such leaders rise above the flood of emotions at work by means of this kind of discrimination. It is as though they are looking at a flooded landscape from a helicopter in the sky. This is not a flight of fancy or the act of running away from the problem. Rather, Krishna points out that one can get better hold of a problem if one can observe from a distance one's own mind with the eye of discrimination. Timeless leaders don't get carried away by the faulty evidence presented by their GPS system. They rather observe the faulty evidence of their misguided minds and make corrections based on the right appraisal of reality. It is like a driver observing a faulty roadmap and deciding to take an alternative route because he realizes that the map does not show the right directions. Thus, timeless leaders alter their own perspective and the perspectives of others.


## CREATING ALTERNATIVE REALITY

Leadership is the art of creating alternative reality. Leaders always bring a refreshing perspective that reframes current reality. Krishna says to Arjuna:

> When it is night for all creatures,
>> The wise one is awake.
>> When they are awake,
>> It is night for the wise leader who sees reality.
>
> *(2.69)*

Reality is not our thoughts and feelings about things. Many of us, for example, think that the Sun rises in the East and sets in the West. In reality, the Sun neither rises nor sets. We on Earth just move closer to the Sun or farther away from it. Most of us do not see reality as it is but rather as we are. This is what Krishna is telling Arjuna: To change your reality, change the mental filters through which you look—your own perspective. Just as a white building when viewed through red glass looks red, similarly, reality as it is can be distorted by the colours of emotions in the mind.

A perspective is more than visual rag–picking. It is much more than passively picking up bits and pieces of information from the surface of reality. A perspective is sight plus insight. Krishna is providing Arjuna with deep insight into his own mind,

What is that insight that Krishna is offering? He is saying, "Listen, Arjuna! If you look at your adversaries in battle with your own prejudices, you are going to make a mess of yourself. Be manly enough to get rid of those prejudices. Drop your emotional baggage and begin to see with the clear light of reason." Krishna is pointing out to Arjuna that as long as he remains in the field of the senses he is likely to be a victim of his narrow perspective. From this narrowness of perspective we often think of the night in terms of the Sun setting, although the Sun has really not set. What is night to our senses is actually a bright day somewhere else in the world. From Krishna's perspective, what Arjuna sees as a gloomy problem on the battlefield is actually a glorious opportunity for him to evolve as a person. In essence, Krishna is inspiring Arjuna to rise above the pairs of opposites:

> Do not get stuck in the duality of pleasure or pain
>   Or in the thought of losing or winning.
>
> *(2.38)*

Krishna is talking about the condition of a mind that is haunted by the pairs of opposites. At the sensory level we get stuck between pleasure and pain. At the mental level we get stuck between gain and loss. Krishna is a timeless leader. He crafts an alternative vision of reality for Arjuna. Krishna says that there is an alternative way to live and lead here. The alternative reality is to avoid being stuck in pain or pleasure, victory or defeat. When one is stuck either in pain or pleasure, suffering is the result. There is a way out of this suffering. This is the way of *mental equipoise* or *sthitapragnya*. In this state of mind one is not affected by circumstances of pain or pleasure or victory or defeat. One just continues to work with equanimity of mind beyond one's immediate gain or loss. In this state of consciousness a leader begins to glimpse a whole new world beyond one's narrow ego-slot. The leader can rise above the pairs of opposites only when he decides to raise the bar of his own motivation from the mundane to the spiritual plane.

## MOTIVATION AND THE MONKEY MIND

To all appearances it would seem that Arjuna has lost his *motivation* to fight. Arjuna's failure to act is not a failure of motive but a failure to see the larger purpose of his action. Those who act out of external motives such as instant sensory pleasure or immediate praise from their superior often end up behaving like monkeys. The monkey mind restlessly shifts from one external stimulus to another. Motivation endures when our motives are more intrinsic and less extrinsic. Intrinsic motivation ceases to be motivation; it becomes *inspiration*. Yet how many of us realize that "motive"-based action often makes monkeys out of us? "I do not believe in motivation," says the maverick president of one of the world's most influential media houses. Why not? "Because any form of motivation makes me dependent on whatever it is that motivates me." Interesting, isn't it?

Motivation is another form of slavery. Many psychologists say that the source of motivation is an unsatisfied need or a deficiency within oneself. An unfulfilled need creates tension in the nervous and the muscular systems. This tension or need produces a drive to seek for goals outside of oneself. Once this goal is achieved the tension is reduced, temporarily. We then move again to satisfy other goals after a while.

We can see that the real object of motivation is not an object at all. It is a state of mental and physical restlessness caused by desire. The thing we desire is in our perception.

The meaning of *pay* or *apple* is not the pay or the apple but only a perception of how it will fulfil our unsatisfied need to be economically or physically satisfied. Desire is limiting perception to focus on an object or a person we desire. Desire is a process of narrowing of perception.

When we narrow our perception often enough, desire becomes restless obsession. Restlessness is a symptom of the monkey mind. How often have we heard the expression: "If you give peanuts as salary, you get monkeys to work for you." Another way of interpreting this is as follows: Monkey minds seek out trivia such as peanuts to reduce their restless nature. The size of the cushion on our chair, or the brand of our car, become the source of motivation. This is surely a form of slavery. It is not the chair or the car that makes one human. It is the human that makes the chair as well as the car!

Krishna's call to Arjuna is a call to raise the bar of motivation so that motivation becomes inspiration. A motorbike or a monkey can't be inspired, but a human being can be inspired. *Inspiration*, as the term suggests, comes from the word *spirit*. When a leader is inspired, he can inspire countless others, like a single flame lighting up a million flames. When an organization's motivation level stagnates at the sensory level of pay, perquisites, and positional power, such an organization begins to stagnate, decay, and die away.

As the commander and leader of the Pandavas it is Arjuna's calling to be inspired by the righteous battle. Unless he is himself inspired, Arjuna cannot marshal his team to fight for the right cause. Therefore, Arjuna's mentor, Krishna, enables him to understand the difference between conventional motivation and true inspiration. Timeless leaders do not motivate followers; they just enable their followers so that they can inspire themselves.

## THE LEADER'S INSPIRATION COMES FROM UNSELFISH WORK

Krishna gives us startling insights into the work-ethic of a leader when he says,

> You have the right to do your work; Arjuna, do not clamour for its fruits.
> Let not the fruit of action be your selfish motive.

*(2.47)*

The entire verse is Krishna's expression of the timeless secret of work, called *nishkama karma* or unselfish work. The four facets of *nishkama karma* are:

1. One has to be fully devoted to the work on hand to get the results.
2. Worrying over results cannot help, as the doer's ego does not determine the results.
3. The cause of the results is not just the selfish motive of the doer but the sum total of many contributions. Therefore one needs to be detached from selfish motives.
4. Work is inevitable and no one can choose to be inactive.

The first facet of *nishkama karma* can be explained by a simple formula:

Unselfish commitment to the process of
work = Best possible results

For Arjuna this implies that victory can come only when he is fully engaged in the battle. Naturally, victory is unlikely to come when the warrior goes half-heartedly into the fight.

Timeless leaders like Krishna realize that results are not separate from the process of action. When all the processes of action are right and timely, results are bound to follow.

The action of the present moment becomes the result in what appears to be the future. The seed of a tree appears to become the fruit in due course of time, although the seed and the fruit belong to one integral process. Leaders understand that the impulse of reward-focussed action becomes a reaction. The present action defined in terms of a future moment in time when the reward is expected becomes the reaction. So, great leaders pay complete attention to the present action without interference from the reward-seeking restless mind.

Then comes the real meaning of *nishkama karma*: To worry over results as Arjuna is doing makes it difficult to be engaged in the present effort. This is because the doer's mind gets preoccupied with anxieties woven around future results. This is like playing baseball with one eye on the scoreboard. It takes away from the focus in the current occupation. Engaged work is full effort minus the ego. This is best illustrated by the story of an apprentice monk who comes to the master to be enlightened:

"How long will it take me to be enlightened," he asks the master restlessly.

"About 10 years," comes the reply.

"What!," the novice cries out in desperation. "What if I double the hours of sitting and triple the hours I am awake, how long will it then take me to be enlightened?"

"About 20 years," answers the master calmly. "When you have only one eye to work with because the other eye is committed to hastening results, it will naturally take double the time."

The next facet of *nishkama karma* is detachment from the results. Why is this so? The psychic energy wasted in attaching it to results can be best utilized when one attaches this energy to the work at hand. The quality of the work at hand will bring about the results in the ultimate analysis. So Krishna is urging Arjuna to detach from the little ego located in our genetic conditioning. This ego is just a provisional starting point of action like the starting mark of an Olympic race. Unless we get off of the starting mark we can't run ahead and win the race.

Timeless leaders understand the value of ego as a temporary starting point in the race of life and not the final destination. What is the final destination of work? Paradoxically, it is the dissolution of the ego in the process of work itself. We have often experienced this phenomenon while we are deeply engaged in work. At some moments of peak performance we enter what may be described as the *flow* state. In this state we seem to be lost in the work. Our experience of the physical body is suspended; time seems to stand still and the spatial boundaries between the worker and the work seem to be dissolved. Many of us have had experiences of these kinds of peak performance states.

In the state of *nishkama karma* our belief in the separate self with ego at the center is suspended and we find for ourselves a greater identity. In losing our ego selves, we find our soul Self. When we view our work from a higher standpoint than just fulfilment of personal ambition our work becomes a great contribution to the larger organization and society. Our personal gain in this is that we also evolve with our work. Our identity gets enriched and expanded. And in the highest point of view our work helps sustain the social and organizational order.

Finally, timeless leaders realize that work itself is inevitable. One cannot avoid work because even as one is lying in bed, the organs of the body and mind are still in work-mode: The heart is beating; the brain is thinking thoughts, and so on. But work that comes from the highest intent of contribution becomes an irresistible force of transformation in the organization and society.

## UNSELFISH WORK LEADS TO EVENNESS OF MIND

Timeless leaders recognize the infallible connection between unselfish work and evenness of mind or *samatvam*. If human evolution is the ultimate goal of all work, then evenness of mind is a more evolved state than that of a frenzied monkey mind swinging up and down the motivational pole. Therefore, says Krishna,

> Perform action, O Arjuna, abandoning attachment.
>> Being steadfast in Yoga and balanced in success and failure.
>> This evenness of mind is called Yoga.
>
> *(2.48)*

There is a parable in the book of Matthew in the New Testament that illustrates the benefit of evenness of mind: A fool constructed a house on sand and when the rains descended and the floods came and the winds blew, the house fell. But a man of wisdom built his house on a rock and as the rains descended and the floods came and the winds blew, the house did not fall for it was built on a rock.

The even mind is like a rock while the monkey mind is like shifting sand. For our work to have enduring value we need evenness of mind. Krishna says that evenness of mind can be achieved when the current of the senses is unplugged from the mind by the power of the intellect. The uneven mind is like shifting sand. Such a mind wavers when faced with crisis. The even mind is like a rock that is serenely anchored in the intellect. The intellect not only calms the mind but also steadies the senses. Under the guidance of the intellect, the senses perform their functions optimally without being driven by the drumbeat of the external world. Most of us are switched on to sensory stimulus automatically without knowing how to switch it off at will. The process of switching off is brought home by a vivid metaphor of a tortoise retracting its limbs:

> When, like the tortoise drawing in its limbs, one can completely withdraw the senses from the sense objects, one is established in wisdom.
>
> *(2.58)*

Just as the tortoise withdraws its physical body into a rock-solid shell, the human intellect has the capacity to withdraw the sensory current into an even mind. A leader who is not steady and even-minded cannot harness the power of the intellect. In the process the quality of decision making in the work suffers. To get the best decisions out of his team, the CEO of one of the world's largest hotel chains remains firm in mind and does not get carried away by any one point of view. He even refuses to nod his head prematurely when one member of the team comes up with a particularly appealing idea. If he were operating with a monkey mind he would have jumped to conclusions immediately upon hearing this idea. This would, however, prompt other people on the team with different ideas to shut up. Their assumption would be that the CEO has already made up his mind about what needs to be done. When the CEOs mind is steady, he can harness a lot more of the team members' thinking for a better-quality decision.

A mind that is carried away by roaming senses also sweeps away understanding and discrimination from the field of action. In another vivid image, Krishna compares such a mind to an unanchored boat tossed about by the wind:

> The mind is carried away by the senses
>> As a boat unanchored can be tossed by the wind.
>
> *(2.67)*

Enslaved by the senses the mind behaves like a direction-less boat and work suffers. Timeless leaders realize that great work happens when there are simultaneously fluidity and steadiness in the thought process. While physical work is the visible external movement of energy, mental work is invisible internal movement of the same energy. The former is the hardware of work while the latter is the software behind the work. Both of these have to be plugged into the "uninterrupted power supply" that comes from the *being* or the soul Self of the leader. Timeless leaders are naturally first switched onto their *being* before they begin to think or act. In doing this their thoughts and actions become deeply integrated. Work flowing from this state goes beyond their selfish, ego-driven interests and becomes an enduring contribution to organizations and societies at large.

## APPLYING INVINCIBLE WISDOM:
## POWERED BY THE INTELLECT AND
## DRIVEN BY UNSELFISHNESS

Krishna presents to Arjuna a comprehensive alternative reality about human capacity. He guides Arjuna on the path of wisdom rather than conventional knowledge.

Timeless leaders know the difference between knowledge and wisdom. Knowledge is like a library: a storehouse of valuable information. Wisdom is the ability to process this knowledge and apply it at the right time and the right place. Knowledge is installed capacity; wisdom is capacity utilized to the right extent.

All the knowledge of the world—that which belongs to the past, present, or future—comes from the sensing, feeling, and thinking mind. The mind is the largest library of the universe. To a leader the world outside is merely the field of application. All the knowledge that Krishna is imparting to Arjuna already exists in Arjuna's mind. Yet Arjuna is unable to use his intellect to harness and utilize this knowledge. Krishna merely helps him to apply this knowledge.

Many of us see a falling apple and think of it as no more than food. Yet, to Sir Isaac Newton, the falling apple presented an occasion to apply his intellect. He studied the phenomenon inside his own mind, made mental calculations, and came to a wise conclusion about the existence of the force of gravity. The knowledge of gravity always existed in Newton's mind just as it did in our minds. Yet, this knowledge remained undiscovered until wisdom prevailed.

The faculty in the human constitution that helps us apply knowledge wisely is called the *intellect*. The result of cultivating the intellect is concentration and steadiness of the mind. The mind is like an ordinary light. It is scattered energy. When concentrated, the mind behaves like a sharp laser light. Concentration helps power to accumulate at the single point of attention. There is no limit to this power. Concentration is the integrating capacity of the mind to a focal point of thought or action. Integration is power; disintegration is weakness.

> There is an old story about a man who was on his death bed. He had several sons who were quarrelling with each other at every pretext. The man was worried that his family would soon come to ruins. So he decided on a course of action. He asked each of his sons to bring a small branch of a tree. Each of them obeyed. Then he asked his eldest son to break a slender branch into two halves. His son did so with ease. Then he put together all the branches and invited all his sons to break the bundle into two. All his sons tried and failed. However, they learnt the power of integration within the family.

Like the old man in the story who integrates his quarrelling sons into a united family, it is the intellect that holds the diverse preoccupations of the mind to one point of occupation. Arjuna's crisis comes from the disconnect between his scattered mind and his weakened intellect. His mental forces—thoughts and feelings—are running amuck. They are tossing him like a rudderless ship. Unable to apply his intellect, he is a nervous wreck. Krishna teaches him how to harness his thoughts and emotions with the guidance of the invincible intellect.

According to Krishna, here is how wisdom works in practice: The human mind is the executive assistant to the CEO called the *intellect*. The mind receives data and perceptions from its inbox tray called the *senses*. Then the mind classifies this information, files it, and sends it to its CEO, the intellect, for its decision. The intellect, based on its own past experiences and its powers of judgement, makes a final decision and conveys it to the mind for implementation. The mind then sends this decision to the outbox tray from where the organs of action pick up the final decision and implement it.

We can see from the above process that the critical role of decision making rests with the intellect. If the intellect is weak, the quality of decision making will be poor and therefore implementation will be poor, too. The real question that Krishna asks is: What will make the intellect become strong? The answer to this question is *unselfish work*. So, here is the timeless principle of applying wisdom: Work unselfishly with an inspired heart and a steady mind that is guided by the intellect.

# SUTRA 3

# KARMA YOGA

## Leaders Enter the Timeless Cycle of Action

Arjuna thinks that the path of knowledge and action are separate. Krishna points out that these two paths are complementary like the two sides of the same coin. Arjuna is looking for a simpler answer. He is not able to reconcile a life of contemplative knowledge and the path of "terrible action" that the war demands. Krishna tells Arjuna that wisdom truly reveals itself in an unselfish action. He points out that action is unavoidable as it is inherent in the three modes of Nature. He reveals to Arjuna the timeless cycle of action in which work is an act of sacrifice for the perpetuation of the cycle. This sutra is an unfolding of *karma yoga*—or the timeless leader's path of enlightened action.

## ARJUNA'S DILEMMA:
## THE WARRIOR AS WORRIER

If you say, O Krishna, that knowledge is superior to action,
Why then do you engage me in such terrible action?

*(3.1)*

Arjuna's dilemma comes straight from his divided mind.
He wants to split his own world into two halves: thought and
action. In many ways, Arjuna is like most leaders who are
caught in the emotional bind where thoughts often do not
translate into action. Many CEOs state this as one of their
usual problems. They say, "I know that I have to urgently act
on a few things that are important to me as well as to the
organization, but I never get around to doing them." Very
typically the sore points of inaction and indecision happen to
be those that require the CEO to go through major emotional upheavals such as life-style changes, turnaround plans,
confronting nonperformance, or bringing negative news to
the organization.

Arjuna is unable to find a way out of the dilemma arising
from his mental confusion. So he says,

Your advice seems inconsistent, O Krishna; show me one
path to follow to the ultimate good.

*(3.2)*

Arjuna is bewildered because his is a binary mind where
the world is divided into black and white. Like most leaders,
Arjuna is confronting an ambiguous situation where there is
no either/or answer. So, Krishna is faced with the challenge
of evolving Arjuna's thought. He is saying to Arjuna, "While
you are trying to think through a problem, do you see that
your thinking is itself the problem?" Arjuna's thinking is very
linear. He is asking Krishna for a straight-arrow answer:

Tell me, Krishna, one thing for certain so that I can follow one line of action.

*(3.2)*

Now Krishna has to rise to this challenge of evolving Arjuna's thought process. Krishna says to Arjuna: "It is not possible to provide a one-point agenda based on linear thinking." Krishna deliberates on the two apparently different paths of contemplation and action for two distinct kinds of people. These paths eventually lead to the same goal of realizing one's true potential. Depending on the temperament of the leader, the paths may vary but the goal is the same. Krishna says,

At the beginning of Time I declared two paths:
    The intuitive path of knowledge of the spirit and the active path of selfless service.

*(3.3)*

There are different strokes for different folks, as they say. Temperamentally, leaders may be classified in two categories: the contemplative and the active. Therefore, to make progress they follow a path that is true to their own nature. Krishna knows that Arjuna is an active warrior by nature. The warrior has temporarily become a worrier—he is inflicted with worries about not being able to do battle. For a warrior it is a matter of shame to be unable to follow a decisive line of action. Arjuna's lapse into inaction is corroding his vitality. Krishna understands this and deftly leads him out of his confusion.

## WORK AND ITS SECRET: ACTION, INACTION, AND EFFORTLESS ACTION

Krishna starts by clearly describing three different faces of work to Arjuna. First he tells Arjuna that no one reaches enlightenment by not performing one's duty. All of us come into this world to make a contribution based on our capabilities. So, merely renouncing action and thinking of enlightenment will never get us there:

> By not performing work you will never find freedom.
>> By giving up action no one attains perfection.
>
> *(3.4)*

Krishna points out that the whole of Nature, including human nature, is nothing but conditioned action. Our hearts beat at specific rhythms, the planets move in their orbits with unerring motion—all of Nature participates in this grand symphony of well-orchestrated action.

> No one can rest even for an instant without action.
>> For one is always made to act by the forces born of Nature.
>
> *(3.5)*

Therefore, merely by being inactive, by restraining the organs of action, one cannot prevent action from happening. One may sit silently in a room and yet be full of noisy, sense-based thoughts—that's only a pretence of silence. In short, Krishna says inaction is nothing but hypocrisy. Arjuna's so-called inaction is also a negative action against the *dharma* of the warrior whose duty it is to act in the battlefield. Arjuna's indecision is also a decision to do nothing about defending his cause. Krishna makes this abundantly clear:

> Just restraining the organs of action yet thinking of sense objects
>> Is nothing more than pretence of renunciation of action.
>
> *(3.6)*

Thus, Krishna establishes that conscious action is far superior to unconscious inaction. He advises Arjuna to perform his obligatory duties. Even sustaining the body through nutrition and exercise so that one can serve the world requires conscious action. By energetic and cheerful performance of one's duty one can move toward true Self-knowledge. Intense and conscious action unleashes the productive potential that is latent in our muscles and in our minds.

> Perform your obligatory action, Arjuna, for action is superior to inaction.
> Even the bare maintenance of the body will not be possible if you are inactive.
>
> *(3.8)*

By diligently performing one's obligatory actions, a leader moves to the next stage of evolution at work—the stage of effortless action. As the leader begins to work with deep attention, work becomes more engaging. Attention makes any work engaging. Work we love to do never tires us. Such work brings us to a state of *naishkarmya* or the experience of effortlessness. At this point, the mind enters a steady-flow state. This peace of mind gives us a sense of our true nature. Therefore, Krishna says that energetic, selfless work gives us a glimpse of who we are. In the state of effortless action, we still work very hard and yet we do not feel the drudgery as our being transcends our physical nature and we reclaim the experience of the higher dimension that is inside us.

Imagine the experience of a gardener who, after a season of backbreaking work, sees the first flower bloom in spring. He stands enraptured as he observes the flower. The gardener has done sincere work so that the flower could bloom. Yet the gardener has not grown the flower—the flower has grown by itself, effortlessly, with the coming of spring. With his body and mind, the gardener has merely created the right conditions for the flower to bloom. This is how effort and effortlessness work together. Although the gardener may think that his effort has grown the flower, in reality the flower grows by its own nature:

> All actions are performed by the modes of Nature.
>> The ignorant, deluded by the ego, thinks, "I am the doer."
>>> *(3.27)*

## KARMA YOGA: WORK AS WORSHIP

Krishna passes on to Arjuna the ultimate secret of karma yoga. He helps Arjuna discover the effortless principle that works spontaneously through us when we are engaged in selfless action. It is not the action itself but the spirit behind the action that makes the action effortless. A cranky old machine cannot achieve frictionless movement until it is greased and oiled properly. The spiritual essence in karma yoga is like this frictionless movement.

To convey the timeless spiritual essence of an action, the ancient psychologists of India often used the word *karmayoga*. This word does not have a literal translation in English. This compound word loosely means "work that is linked with the transcendental spirit." My futile search for an equivalent expression in English has prompted me to coin a new word, *workship.* Workship literally means "work as worship." More explicitly, this phrase signifies that when work is done in the spirit of worship, the quality of the work undergoes a metamorphosis. As a result, even ordinary work is transformed from a mere chore to work of an extraordinary dimension.

Let us illustrate this with the following example: Three teachers who teach history in different schools are asked the same question: What is your present job? The first one replies, "I don't do very much. I just teach history to schoolchildren." The second teacher thinks a little more deeply and says, "I am in the business of education." The third teacher, in response to the same question, looks straight into the eyes of the questioner and in an inspired voice says, "I am shaping the destiny of the nation. I teach young minds how they can make history."

All three teachers are dealing with the same reality—teaching history to schoolchildren. Yet the spirit in which they approach their work transforms the mundane reality of their job.

It is this transformational power of the spirit of our work that leads us to the concept of workship. The English word *worship* literally means "reverence and respect paid to God." The object of our reverence and respect is not an object at all, but is really the ultimate spiritual expression of the highest, the mightiest, and the biggest entity in our conception, which we describe as God. Similarly, the objective of our work grows bigger and bigger as we lend our spirit to it. We begin to treat our work with greater reverence and respect until a point is reached when our work becomes an expression of our pure spirit. There is something of the divine perfection in this kind of work. It is then that our work becomes workship. The mystic poet of Persia, Jelaluddin Rumi, expressed the experience of *workship* in brilliant poetry:

> I feel like the ground astonished
> at what the sky's spirit has brought to it. What I know
> is growing inside me. Rain makes
> every molecule pregnant with a mystery.
>> *(Coleman Barks,* The Essential Rumi, *HarperCollins,*
>> *New York, 1995)*

Krishna defines *workship* as the performance of action for the unfolding of the spirit of our being toward greater perfection and a higher state of consciousness. This state of perfection is not outside ourselves but is an implicit state of our being. Thus, workship implies the following:

Workers are fundamentally spiritual beings involved in a human experience; they are more than human resources looking for a paycheck and a pat on the back. There is an autonomous self-existent spiritual dimension to the human constitution. Our body-mind-senses framework is but a partial expression of our spiritual wholeness. This wholeness is described as the state of *poornatwa* or the fullness of our spiritual being. *Poornatwa* is a heightened awareness of our own reality.

The ultimate goal of all work is to unfold the *poornatwa* of a human being. Thus, the value of work is understood in terms of human development and not merely material output. Max DePree, a retired CEO of Herman Miller, the well-known office furniture company, rightly says that the measure of individuals—and hence of corporations—is the extent to which we struggle to complete ourselves. Our value, then, can be described as the energy we devote to living up to our complete potential.

The spirit of leaders' actions springs from the nature of their being and its inner foundation in their consciousness. Sri Krishna explains this process of the spiritualization of action as he urges Arjuna: "Reclaim your being, be reborn into the spirit, and by that new birth proceed with the action to which the spirit within has appointed you."

In workship, the focus of the leader's action changes from becoming, which is a function of external recognition such as pay or promotion, to being, which is a function of consciousness.

## THE *YAJNA* SPIRIT: DISCOVERING THE TIMELESS CYCLE OF WORK

Timeless leaders do not see their work as mere activity but rather as a calling. For them work is a means of transformation of consciousness. Krishna draws Arjuna's attention to the timeless cycle of work where all action is a sacrifice for a higher cause:

> From food comes forth beings; from rain food is produced;
>> From sacrifice arises rain, and sacrifice is born of action.
>>> *(3.14)*

In the cosmic wheel of work, food creates all forms on Earth. But food itself is grown because of the rain showers that replenish Earth. Rain is the result of the sacrifice of water vapour here on Earth, and sacrifice is the result of work on Earth. This is the spirit of *yajna*—the cosmic wheel of work.

In simple language, *yajna* is self-sacrificing work in the spirit of welfare for all. The two fundamental aspects of *yajna* are sacrifice and service. This is the basis of the ecological consciousness of work that sustains the universe. Krishna seems to say to Arjuna, "You are much larger than you think. You can experience this when you do work in the spirit of *yajna*. You can see the interdependent universe that is connected by work." *Yajna* does not limit us to our human experience but transports us to a much larger dimension. We come to realize that even by removing a single stone in our backyard we are altering the face of Earth.

Timeless leaders have a clear comprehension of the *yajna* spirit—they give before they take. By giving without expectation they spontaneously create space for receiving from a bountiful and interconnected universe. A leader's whole life is a *yajna*. This is the very principle behind one's growth as a person. By forgetting their own narrow concerns and in being of service to others, leaders begin to live in their consciousness the timeless cycle of work.

*Sacrifice* is thus a critical dimension of leadership work. This word has acquired a negative connotation in everyday usage. However, the sacrifice that we are talking about in the context of leadership work does not diminish the self but extends the boundary of the self by giving up the lower for the cause of the higher. Krishna in the *Bhagavad Gita* talks about psychological sacrifice in terms of self-control and self-discipline, which leads to higher Self-evolution and Self-knowledge. For instance, a leader who sacrifices small pleasures on the way to his workplace and arrives there on time every day acquires the virtue of punctuality, which benefits not only himself but also his organization.

Character and credibility acquired through sacrifice do not diminish over time like material resources. They obey the law of abundance by growing in time and spreading in space. The many small sacrifices of the leader eventually add up to a subtle power—the power of a purpose-filled life. A life of purpose engages with a higher law of Nature, a law that transcends the life of a single human being and embraces humanity at large. Krishna's message to Arjuna is: "Have a great purpose to work for, a purpose larger than your personal agenda. This is the way to make life significant. When you work in the spirit of *yajna* your contribution will overflow the span of a lifetime and survive even your physical death."

## *SWADHARMA*: THE CASE FOR RIGHTEOUS ACTION

The privilege of leadership comes with enormous responsibility. Leaders have to live not only for themselves but also for others who choose to follow them. This is a timeless psychological truth: Most men and women imitate what their leaders do. Krishna is arousing Arjuna to accept the fact that as the greatest living warrior of his time, it is Arjuna's responsibility to leave a legacy of bravery for others to emulate:

> Whatever the leader does, the other men imitate;
>> Whatever he sets up as standard, the others emulate.
>
> *(3.21)*

In this, a leader's work is no different from parenting. Parents not only have to live their own lives but also have to live for their children. Like parents, leaders touch the generations that follow them. Often, children don't do what their parents say—they do what their parents do. It is the leader's actions rather than his speeches that followers imitate.

Timeless leaders also set standards that mould the culture of a country or an organization. Their personal life-script becomes the collective script. How do leaders therefore evolve a personal script that is so powerful as to affect the collective behaviour of a large number of people? How do the lives of leaders like Krishna, Gandhi, Buddha, or Christ hold sway over large masses way beyond their lifetimes? According to Krishna, a leader is able to move the masses because he is fully able to live his *swadharma* or the law of his being:

> It is better to die doing one's own dharma,
> For another's dharma is fraught with fear.
>
> *(3.35)*

*Swadharma* is nothing but the law of one's being. A leader is able to live his *swadharma* when he knows both his strengths and his weaknesses but is yet able to act from his strengths. Leaders gain power from profound self-knowledge and complete self-acceptance. When they are completely comfortable with who they are, leaders are able to accept others as they are.

Righteousness is another expression of *swadharma*. Ordinarily, *righteousness* means ethically right action. Righteous action, however, is not merely superficial morality. In its true sense, righteous action means acting according to the law of one's being. Righteous action also implies that the means used for the performance of action are as important as achieving the end results. Thus, doing the right thing assumes as much importance as doing the thing right. In *worship*, an action has no value in itself; it takes its value from the force it represents. All action has a certain purpose behind it. Leadership action is a statement of leadership purpose. In the words of Swami Vivekananda, one of India's greatest spiritual leaders, "Work is inevitable; it must be so. But we must work for the right purpose."

The *dharma* of the self broadly defines the purpose of one's life. For example, it is the *dharma* of the apple tree to produce apples. To expect an apple tree to produce mangoes would be contrary to its *swadharma*. There are several interpretations of the word *dharma*, all of which may help us in understanding what righteousness is all about. One meaning of *dharma* is the intrinsic nature of all animate and inanimate matter that obeys Nature's laws. Yet another meaning of *dharma* is "religion." *Dharma* also means "right conduct." The classic advice given by Krishna to Arjuna to "act according to your *dharma*" conveys the multiple meanings of righteous action. The *Brihadaranyaka Upanishad* describes the link between action and *swadharma* in memorable poetry:

> You are what your deepest nature is.
> As your nature, so is your will.
> As your will is, so is your deed.
> As your deed is, so is your destiny.

> (Brihadaranyaka Upanishad)

## WORK AS A MEANS OF REALIZING WHO WE ARE

In the ordinary state of consciousness it is difficult for us to think of work as a sacrifice. It is equally difficult for us to work unselfishly. Krishna understands this, so he makes it simpler for Arjuna. Dedicate the results of all your actions to a higher consciousness (in this case, Krishna). If Arjuna is able to do it, he will be free from the feverish anxiety that comes from anticipating the results of an action. Thus free, Arjuna will be able to gain access to his immortal soul-Self.

Dedicating the fruits of all actions to me, with mind centered
on the Self, from desire and ego, fight free from mental fever.

*(3.30)*

This immortal Self is nothing but our soul. The mind is
subtler than the body, and the intellect is subtler than the
mind, but the soul is the most subtle aspect of our identity.
The soul is covered by desire:

As a fire is covered by smoke, as a mirror by dust,
    As an embryo is enveloped by the womb, so the soul is
veiled in desire.

*(3.38)*

Desire is nothing but a feverish mind that can be calmed
down by working without anxiety or fuss. When we are able
to dedicate our work to a higher cause we get the strength to
work with peace and calmness. When we are out of the gravi-
tational pull of desire, we are like a spacecraft that has
acquired enough escape velocity to move effortlessly in space.
Dedicated, desire-less work without fever or fuss gives us the
speed of clarity. When a leader accesses clarity of soul at work,
his work enters the timeless cycle of action.

# SUTRA 4

---

# TIMELESS LEADERS PURSUE PURPOSE AS THE SOURCE OF SUPREME POWER

Arjuna is still in doubt about whether the words of Krishna, inspiring though they are, have any precedence. Arjuna is looking for more evidence in support of what Krishna has shared with him thus far. Krishna brings a compelling endorsement from the ancient practices of the sage-kings. He convinces Arjuna that all he has said so far is a reiteration of timeless *yoga*—the ancient science of supreme power practiced by many leaders in the past. This is the grand portal through which all leaders must pass if they wish to achieve the supreme power of enlightened Self.

## *RAJARSHI:* THE LEADER AS SAGE

The ideal of the sage-king as the leader of a community is as ancient as the mountains. Krishna assures Arjuna that his teachings are nothing new. The mystical tradition of yoga that he is talking about has sustained leadership culture for thousands of years. Sometimes this tradition is forgotten with the lapse of time and is buried in the dust of human history. From time to time, a leader like Buddha or Krishna resurrects it from hoary history to embody this glorious tradition. Krishna said:

> Thus handed down in a line of succession, the royal sages knew this yoga; this yoga, by long lapse of time, declined in this world, O Arjuna.
>
> *(4.2)*

Krishna traces the long line of succession through which this teaching has gone: "I taught this yoga to the Sun-god Vivisan. Vivisan taught this to his son, Manu, the originator of mankind. Manu in turn taught this to his son, Ikshvaku, a mighty king of his time." As we can see, Krishna traces the lineage of the yoga tradition to the cosmic cycle beginning with the Sun. The Sun is a metaphor for energy and illumination. The Sun brings about the synthesis of terrestrial energy and celestial light. This is also what the yoga tradition stands for: the combination of Earth and Heaven, the human and the divine, and of the *raja* and the *rishi* as in the word *rajarshi*.

This ancient tradition of yoga is perennial. Like the Sun, it energises and illumines us several lifetimes. Yet when the Sun seemingly sets before our eyes on the horizon we assume that the Sun is gone. In reality, the Sun is still there—only a little obscured from our vision. As the Sun rises again the next morning, we are reassured of its presence.

Yoga is the science of reality: the unity of human life with the divine light. According to the yoga tradition, the royal sage or the *rajarshi* stands for this unity. One part of *rajarshi* is *raja* or king, who embodies power. The other part of *rajarshi* is the *rishi* or the sage, who stands for transcendental wisdom. *Rajarshi* is nothing but the timeless principle through which power is utilized for the purpose of evolution of humankind.

The *rajarshi* model of timeless leadership tells us that exercise of power that is not in harmony with the greater purpose of life is fraught with danger. The *raja* or the wielder of power has to aspire to the wisdom of a *rishi*. We have seen many examples of the collapse of organizations and we have witnessed one of the world's most crippling economic recessions because of misuse of power. We can trace each of these crises to the divorce of the *raja* from the *rishi*.

If a leader holds or accepts power that exceeds his wisdom, the entire organization is bound to suffer. The plight of the many resource-rich countries around the world that are struggling with poverty, environmental crises, and exploitation of men, women, and children is witness to what happens when the *raja* has lost connection with the *rishi*.

Power devoid of purpose inebriates the holder as well as the beholder. The leader who holds power often forgets that this power is held only as a trust on behalf of the followers. Those followers who behold power from the sidelines enter into a relationship of dependence on the power holder. They outsource their own power to a despotic leader. Very often this kind of relationship breeds coteries, power lobbies, and vicious cartels.

Krishna models for Arjuna the way of wielding power with responsibility. Although he himself is the embodiment of divine power, Krishna addresses Arjuna as a friend and follower:

> The secret of this teaching is profound. I have explained it
> to you today because you are my friend and devotee.
>
> *(4.3)*

In doing so, Krishna clarifies that a leader is a friend and partner. He is a guide by the side rather than a sage on a stage.

The leader as *rajarshi* derives his power from this partnership. This is a model that is built on deep democracy. Krishna and Arjuna are friends in spirit, although one is a master and the other a devotee based on their evolutionary history.

## THE MANY FACES OF THE SUPREME POWER

Krishna says leaders have many ways of accessing the supreme power depending on who they are on the scale of human evolution. The supreme power, like electricity, is impersonal. One can use electricity for heating an iron or for cooling a refrigerator or for revolving the blades of a fan. Electricity is impersonal—it neither cools nor heats up nor revolves. It is the nature of the device that uses electricity that does all the things. In a similar vein, the supreme power that Krishna embodies makes itself available to all kinds of leaders with differing evolutionary urges. Some leaders seek the power of fame, some seek money, others seek control over others, and a handful seek to empower others. Krishna helps all to fulfill their individual urges:

> I manifest my power in all without prejudice.
>> In whatever form they invoke me, I serve them.
>>> *(4.11)*

The supreme power therefore makes itself available to a leader in a measure that is in keeping with the temperament of the leader. Power is not just a function of the position that a leader holds but also a function of his mental disposition. There are leaders who seek money. For them, money is the ultimate deity. They dedicate themselves to the pursuit of money in the same way a devotee dedicates himself to his chosen deity. Then there are leaders who seek fame. They feed on the attention of others and devote their entire lives to chasing fame. Some leaders go to the extreme of seeking posthumous fame. They are fussy about where they will be buried and what will be written on their tombstones.

Power seekers in the material universe become disillusioned with their pursuit. This happens because material power, whether provided by money or fame, is subject to change. Such power is very transient. The material power of the world is experienced by the sensory motor nerves in the leader's body-mind. Repeated exposure to the same stimulus causes the sensory motor nerves to learn to adapt and so they no longer bring the same intensity of experience. Seeking outward for more stimulus of the same kind does not bring the same intensity of the response. The constantly outgoing senses follow the law of diminishing returns. When the pleasures of the senses diminish the mind turns inward rather than outward. This is a turning point for many leaders, who now begin to look inward. At this point, the outbound *raja* (*the power of sensory energy*) turns toward the inbound *rishi* (*the power of intellect that pulls the mind inward in the direction of the soul Self*). Then the worldly power of the *raja* unites with the soul power of *rishi*. Thus the power of the world begins to be guided by the power of the Self. The following story illustrates the point:

Alexander was camping on the border of the Indian subcontinent. He had marched triumphantly over half the world, conquering and subjugating one kingdom after another in fierce battles. In a sense, he was like the CEO of a multinational corporation battling local competitors, doing mergers and acquisitions, and grabbing market share. In some places, he struck strategic alliances with local chieftains and held control. In other countries, he confronted his adversaries and raided their territories.

On the threshold of his passage to India, however, Alexander encountered a strange man. This man, dressed in a loincloth, would meditate for hours in a secluded place near

Alexander's camp. For several days, Alexander saw this sage seated in a lotus position while looking toward the horizon. To Alexander, this sage seemed like a lazy man, a recluse who had dropped out of everyday life. One day, the great warrior, unable to contain his curiosity, approached the sage and asked, "Don't you have anything to do besides sitting and dreaming?"

The sage sat there unmoved.

"I see you every morning, evening, and afternoon in the same place. You have not moved an inch. You must be a terrible fellow!"

The sage did not speak a word.

"Tell me, what is your goal in life?" demanded Alexander, exasperated.

The sage smiled a little and said, "Great warrior, you must first tell me about your goal in life before I tell you mine."

Outraged, Alexander thundered, "Don't you know I am Alexander? I am out to conquer the world."

"What do you want to do after you have conquered the world?" the sage asked.

"I will then possess all the gold and all the elephants and horses in the world," said Alexander, his lips curling in disdain.

"And then?" the sage asked.

"Then I will have all men as my slaves."

"And then?"

"Then I will have all the women to serve me."

"And then?"

"Then I will sit on my throne, relax, and enjoy myself."

The sage smiled. "Sir, that is precisely what I am doing right now," he said. "Why are you bothering me? Please leave me alone and go ahead with your conquests."

Both Alexander and the sage are leaders who envision their world in the light of their own consciousness. Alexander seeks fulfilment in the conquest of the outward world of form and phenomenon. The sage searches for peace in the inner domain of subjective experience.

Alexander's consciousness, like that of Arjuna, experiences the world as a battlefield, whereas the sage's consciousness, like that of Krishna, experiences the same world as the field of Self-realization. Alexander thinks, "How much more do I need to be happy?" while the sage ponders, "How much less can I have and still be happy?" Human motivation for power is in constant oscillation between these two questions as they ring in our consciousness: "How much more do I need to be happy?" and "How much less can I have and still be happy?" The sage and Alexander, like Krishna and Arjuna, live within all of us. They represent the two fundamental states of human consciousness. Together they constitute the profile of *rajarshi*, the royal sage.

## TWENTY-FOUR-HOUR LEADERSHIP

Timeless leadership is a lifelong journey, not toward power but toward perfection. In this journey a leader must ceaselessly deal with the rigours of self-conquest.

As we can see, Arjuna's fight is really not with his enemies but with himself. The real warrior has to subdue the waves of negative emotions that arise in him. He must learn to do battle against his own nervous impulses. Leadership is not a nine-to-five affair. It is a 24/7/365 work of a lifetime. Why is that so? Leadership is an evolving process that embraces the whole of life. Arjuna, the leader, cannot say that he will be a hero at home but a nervous wreck on the battlefield. He must be consistent in his personal evolution whether at home or at war. A leader is much more than a boss. An office boss is a static portfolio of competencies; a leader is a dynamo of evolving life. A leader is like magnetism or gravity, which works 24 hours a day without fail.

Leadership, as we discovered earlier, is not a position that someone occupies for a certain number of hours a day. Leadership is rather a disposition, a way of living in the world.

Arjuna is learning to lead. As a learner he humbles himself before his mentor, Krishna. He looks for inspiration while in despair and despondency. One of the unfailing traits of leaders who pursue purpose is humility. Humility is not about putting on an act. Humility is the ability to be in a learning mode all the time—24 hours a day, 7 days a week, and 365 days a year. When a leader is humble he does not think any less of himself. He just thinks of himself less. He annihilates his egocentric actions in the perennial fire of self-awakening:

> Just as a flaming fire reduces
>> Wood to ashes, Arjuna,
>> So the fire of wisdom
>> Reduces all egotistic actions to ashes.
>
> *(4.37)*

In the light of his awakening, the leader gains voluntary control over his sense organs. He is easily able to withdraw his senses from sense objects. His actions no longer remain conditioned by past memory or desire. Very soon, the seeker of wisdom becomes the seer. This seer is the perennial observer of our actions who is not identified with any of these actions. Most of the involuntary actions taking place inside our body, such as digestion, circulation, and the actions of our immune system, happen under the vigil of this observer or seer within us. When a leader is awakened, even the smallest of his thoughts and the minutest of his actions come under the supervision of this observer.

From the point of view of the observer all those deep-rooted attachments to egotistic actions fall away. The flaming fire of the seer dispels the delusion of separateness of the leader from the followers. This awakening shows in the leader's capacity to understand multiple points of view. The leader expands his span of attention from merely the nine-to-five day into the twenty-four-hour-a-day journey of awakening to one's own Self.

## THE RETURN OF THE *RISHI*

The *rishi* is the seer of the whole; the *rishi* is the eternal traveller. The *rishi* consciousness is what timeless leaders aspire to while they pursue purpose. Whenever an organization, a country, or a culture stumbles on the blind materialism that oppresses the human spirit, the *rishi* returns in our consciousness to restore order. Krishna announces the return of the *rishi* in these very prophetic lines:

> For the protection of virtue
> > And for destruction of evil
> > To set the standards of righteousness
> > I appear in age after age.

*(4.8)*

The *rishi* consciousness lies dormant in the evolutionary history of human beings. It becomes evident through the presence of the timeless leader in human form in certain times. A Buddha, a Christ, or a Krishna arises when human conduct strays away from those virtues that sustain evolution.

Krishna reveals his timeless appearance in multiple incarnations to protect virtue and set standards of righteousness. The return of the *rishi* is necessary to restore those timeless human values such as Love, Truth, and Justice that often get neglected as the quest for material success grips our collective consciousness. The fall of the Roman and the Greek civilizations was brought about by the decline of these eternal values. The rise of Japan from the ashes of the war was made possible by the resurrection of those selfless, communitarian values.

We can see the return of the *rishi* consciousness in the transformation and turnaround of organizations around the world. Organizations often fall prey to their own inertia and become directionless. In these hard times we have seen a *rishi* leader come forth and transform such an organization into a vibrant entity.

It is the leader's characteristic humility despite high performance that underlines the *rishi* consciousness. Two examples of *rishi* leaders were J.R.D. Tata of India and Konosuke Matsushita of Japan. J.R.D. Tata created the industrial empire of the Tatas in India. Yet, when he died, his managers were surprised to see that even as the head of an empire he had lived in a rented house and had very little in the way of personal property. J.R.D. Tata believed in the principle of trusteeship. A leader committed to trusteeship holds in trust the wealth of an organization for the benefit of the community rather than for his personal consumption.

While inspecting a blast furnace in the steel city of Jamshedpur in eastern India, J.R.D. Tata was briefed by an engineer about the features of an expensive blast furnace that was installed with the help of technology imported from Europe. Mr. Tata was not very keen on the technical details. He merely asked the engineer: "Have you thought about the poor workman who is going to operate the blast furnace? Have you thought of how he would feel working near a furnace that generates so much heat?"

The legendary Konosuke Matsushita of the Panasonic brand in Japan allowed his employees to continue to work in one of his factories despite postwar depression and this company incurring losses. Fired by the faith Matsushita had in their abilities, his workers went out into the streets of Osaka and Tokyo to sell the products of the company. His workers eventually turned this company around because their leader had trusted them to do so. Matsushita then gave the company to them, as he had earlier promised. When asked what made the turnaround possible, Matsushita simply said, "I just held up an umbrella when it was raining."

All *rajarshis*, whether they are corporate leaders or leaders in other walks of life, are like waves in the vast ocean of the omnipresent Spirit. They liberate organizations from meaningless formalities and the wickedness of vested interests. The return of the *rishi* is the call of the ocean to the waves. Just as every wave longs to return to the ocean, every timeless leader strives to return to the source of perennial inspiration and rejuvenation in the spirit. The apparent collision of waveforms is nothing but the conflict of individual identities within the narrow boundaries of the organizational ego. The leader as the *rishi* breaks free from these confining boundaries and the prison of these formalities to ascend to the ever-awake and ever-free light and life.

# SUTRA 5

## LEADERSHIP IS THE ART OF UNDOING

## The State of Detached Engagement

Arjuna wants to know which of the paths will lead to the ultimate goal of life: performance of duty or renunciation of action. "Why praise renunciation and at the same time urge me to perform one action or the other?" Arjuna is asking whether he shall fight or seek peace. Krishna says that these are not conflicting but complementary—Arjuna will find peace only when he fights without being a fighter. This is a paradox Arjuna is not able to unravel. Arjuna is wondering why Krishna is urging him to fight while advocating renunciation at the same time. Krishna makes it clear that when action is unselfish, renunciation and performance of action mean the same thing. Thus, he initiates Arjuna into one of the greatest insights into action philosophy: Be totally engaged in whatever you have to do but detach your ego from the illusion of doer-ship. Krishna clarifies further: It is Nature that acts through us by engaging our sense organs in the world. Our innermost soul Self does nothing at all. The Self merely observes as the senses get busy at work: seeing, listening, eating, talking, breathing, and acting. The Self is like the CEO who keenly observes while all the other executives in his organization execute with flawless precision. Krishna points out to Arjuna the ultimate goal of detached engagement: a state of being in the zone of equanimity and unshakable equilibrium even in the middle of hectic activity.

## HOW ANCHORS OF THE PAST HINDER PERFORMANCE

The leader was taking his entire team on a river cruise to a distant island in order to celebrate the company's phenomenal performance in the last quarter. The engine of the ship started in full throttle. The entire cruise ship was hired by the company. The ship was decorated with glittering lights and colorful balloons soared over the deck. Frothing champagne flowed as freely as the river. There was merriment all around. There was mutual backslapping and all that chatter about how we did this and how we did that! Dinner was, as expected, a gala affair. Hours passed by in revelry and not until well past midnight had the drunken people on board noticed that the ship had not moved at all from the harbour. How could it? The crew had forgotten to remove the ship's anchor.

Organizations that are tethered to the past are no different from a ship that has forgotten to lift its anchor. Past performance, past glory, past habits—all of them have the potential to destroy our work. While we are held captive by our past we are not able to move on and be fully engaged with the work at hand. The result is that we daydream, hallucinate, and relive the fears and anxieties of the past. As a result, what suffers is the quality and efficiency of the present.

Arjuna's plight is that he is anchored to the emotions and memories of past experiences. He is unable to move on and engage with the battle at hand. Krishna's solution to this dilemma is to tell Arjuna to steer clear of the bondage of the past. He urges Arjuna to observe the twin emotions of aversion and craving: aversion for unpleasant memories of the past and craving for a projected future. Both these emotions hold us back from performance of our actions in the present moment. Krishna points out to Arjuna that there is a psychological state beyond these dual emotions: the state of the *witness.* The drunken men and women on board the cruise ship have forgotten to witness that the ship they are on is still anchored such that it cannot move forward. If one needs to take a step forward, one must lift one's foot. One can do that only when one is awake and liberated from one's location in the past.

What is the nature of that psychological state of being liberated? Krishna describes this as a state of renunciation in action. A mind that is not glued to past action flows freely without reactions from the past:

> One who neither hates nor desires is free from the pairs of opposites;
>> O mighty-armed Arjuna, he is liberated from bondage.
>
> *(5.3)*

There are two stubborn anchors of the mind that prevent the ship of our lives from moving forward: likes and dislikes. Likes and dislikes come from conditioned memories of the past. When the leader's decisions are based on personal likes and dislikes his actions are seen as biased by his followers. As the leader goes beyond likes and dislikes he lifts his anchors from the past and begins to live in the present moment. The present is free from the noises of the past and voices of the future. His hatred for the past actions of his adventures and his desire for a just resolution cloud Arjuna's consciousness. Hates and desires are like wild dogs that keep barking at us from our past. The timeless leader stops paying heed to the voices of the past and is thus liberated from bondage to them.

## THE ART OF DETACHED INVOLVEMENT

> Mentally renouncing all actions and fully self-controlled the embodied soul
>> Remains blissfully seated in the body of nine gates.
>
> *(5.13)*

A certain corporate leader was invited to an alumni reunion dinner. As he arrived at the meeting he was happy to see familiar faces. Most of his classmates from the business school had made a mark in their lives. Almost everybody was somebody in the corporate pecking order, except for one classmate whom the leader recognized as the one who had dropped out of the rat-race. They had all heard about him. An achiever with high potential, he had decided to become a monk. The leader was curious to know how his life had progressed. This man, whose name was Ray, had a cheerful disposition. The leader walked up and introduced himself, and said, "Do you recognize me, Ray? We went to school together." Ray nodded his head in acknowledgement. "Why did you give up on a great career, Ray?," the CEO enquired. "Wasn't money important to you at that stage in life?" Ray quietly told his friend that there were more important drivers for him than just money. The leader laughed, pretty much dismissing Ray as too idealistic.

After the dinner the leader invited Ray to spend the night in his palatial apartment on a small island off the mainland. They wanted to catch up on how their lives had shaped up after all these years. They went to a ferry terminal to get on the ferryboat that would take them to the island. As luck would have it, the ferry service was closed as it was well past the time for scheduled service. The CEO asked the last ferryboat captain whether he would be willing to take them even though it was past his scheduled duty hours. The captain shook his head reluctantly. The leader took out a bunch of currency notes from his wallet and asked whether that pile of money would make the captain change his mind. Driven by the incentive of making a fast buck the captain agreed to take them to the island.

While they were sailing toward the island the CEO teased his monk friend: "What good is your renunciation when money can get work done so easily? Do you think we could have reached our palace tonight if I did not have the money to throw at the ferryman?" This time Ray had the last laugh. "Yes, I agree with you. Money is a powerful force. But it isn't half as powerful when you possess it as when you *dispossess* it. The moment you gave away the money to the ferryman it began to work!"

To practice the art of detached involvement is to be able to govern the senses at will. Our senses have a tendency to be easily attached to the most trivial of things. But that is not really the problem; the real problem begins when we are not able to detach our senses with equal ease. When leaders are able to govern their senses by withdrawing the needy acquisitive mind from sensory engagement, they practise detached involvement. Leaders achieve this through the regular practice of reflection. Reflection brings about equality of vision.

## EVOLVING TO THE EQUALITY OF VISION

Timeless leaders strive constantly to equalize their vision. This is crucial if one wishes to succeed in leading people. When leaders do not have equality of vision they end up promoting partiality, prejudice, and cliques, which ruin organizations. Followers expect their leaders to be fair and just in their treatment of them. Each time a leader betrays a bias toward someone or a certain class of people, he violates the trust that people have placed in him. The hallmark of wisdom in a leader is the power to see with an equitable eye. Krishna says:

> Learned men see with an equal eye
> > Someone who is equally learned,
> > a cow, an elephant, a dog,
> > and even an outcaste scavenger.
>
> *(5.18)*

One way leaders demonstrate their lack of equality of vision is when they move away from people they dislike. When they meet someone they dislike they get unduly perturbed. The Dalai Lama has a wonderful method of teaching people how to equalize their vision. He would first ask you to close your eyes and visualize the face of a person that you intensely like and observe the feelings that arise as a result. Then he would ask you to visualize the face of a person that you intensely dislike and observe whatever feelings arise in you. Finally, you would be asked to visualize the face of a person that you neither like nor dislike and observe the feelings that this person evokes in you. When all three feeling states eventually become the same, you can claim to have understood the equality of vision.

Striving toward the equality of vision requires reconditioning the nervous system to accept likes and dislikes without becoming unduly agitated. This can be achieved with intense self-observation and practice in meditation. Where does equality of vision come from? It comes from the ability to see the same human spirit dispersed in several forms across the dividing lines of caste, creed, designations, or degrees of accomplishment. When our meditation deepens we are able to experience this unity in divinity on an everyday basis.

One world leader who has cultivated this singularity of vision is Nelson Mandela. In his life and work he lived the truth of the ancient Bantu saying *umuntu ngumuntu ngabantu*—we are people through other people. And he saw from his ancient African wisdom, and from his country's violent history, the inevitability of the interdependence of the human society. He also understood that in the human context the shared higher ground of the human spirit is greater and more enduring than the differences that divide. Mandela emerged as a man with an equality of vision. He created the ideal of a "rainbow nation" where a diversity of people and cultures could be held together in the same fabric of light and life.

Another leader who led through unity of vision was Mohammad Yunus of the Grameen Bank in Bangaladesh. He dispelled a stubbornly held banking myth that the poor are less reliable than the rich when it comes to repaying bank loans. Where conventional bankers brought lawyers into their transactions, Yunus brought trust. Where conventional banks lent money mostly to men, Yunus lent money to the poorest of women. He believed that the poor women of Bangaladesh's village were just as trustworthy as their rich male counterparts. He was proved right. Those poorest-of-the-poor women showed themselves to be more trustworthy in repayment of loans than the more affluent men. Yunus talks from his experience about the conventional mindsets that prevent leaders from achieving unity of vision:

> My greatest challenge has been to change the mindset of people. Mindsets play strange tricks on us. We see things the way our minds have instructed our eyes to see.

Mindsets get in the way of equalizing vision. The challenge before Krishna is to help Arjuna see beyond the barriers of his mindset. Arjuna cannot see with clarity because his vision is obstructed by his mindset, which looks only at the surface of reality and jumps to conclusions. Krishna now urges Arjuna to consider how leaders can win the battle between the pure mind rooted in the equality of vision and the impure mindset.

# THE ART OF UNDOING

Leadership as we know it has become associated with frantic action and dramatic results. For most people, leadership is nothing more than *doer*-ship. To talk about leadership in terms of "what the leader has done" is to tell only half of the story. The other half of the story consists of what the leader has *undone*. The most potent leaders of this world, such as Gandhi or Martin Luther King Jr., were busy undoing the ignorance of the past ways of life, whether in the form of violence entrenched in the mind or racial discrimination. These leaders had to first change their own, and then, by their influence, their followers' mindsets. Similarly, Arjuna's problem as a warrior is not merely about his inability to *do battle*. Rather, his problem is more about his ability to change his mindset by undoing the past.

As change agents leaders have to embrace the constant tug-of-war between the past and the future. When a leader's personality is programmed by his past actions, his energy is trapped in time. His future becomes only a recycled past, as the following story illustrates.

A high-profile CEO was addicted to his extravagant lifestyle and the large-scale splurging of money on projects that were thoughtlessly launched. It was the time of a severe economic downturn, and as the markets tumbled the CEO sunk his company and ultimately lost his job. As is usually the case, when the CEO lost all his money and his assets, his friends deserted him one after another.

Unable to bear his sorrow, the CEO sought the counsel of a wise teacher. He asked, almost in tears, "What will happen to me? I have no job, no money, and no friends." The teacher said, "Do not worry, everything will be all right soon—it will be business as usual for you again." Encouraged by the teacher's remark and a with glimmer of hope in his eyes, the CEO asked, "Will I be rich again?" The teacher replied, "Well, I do not want to predict that far. All I can assure you is that you will very soon get used to being poor and friendless."

Like the CEO in the story, Arjuna is getting used to his helplessness. Just as the CEO does not examine the mindset of extravagance and blind speculative instinct that has led to his downfall, Arjuna does not examine the undercurrent of guilt and despondency that is leading to his failure to act. The problem is not Arjuna's inaction but rather his unawareness of the mental chatter that is corroding his vitality. A timeless leader refuses to get bogged down by such unintelligent mental chatter. He knows that it would soon drain his energy.

Krishna teaches Arjuna how to discipline the mind by renouncing the false notion that his mental chatter is the agency of action:

> Seeing, hearing, touching, smelling,
>     Eating, walking, sleeping, breathing,
>     The disciplined man who knows reality
>     Should think, "I do nothing at all."
>
> *(5.8)*

This is the process of inspired dis-identification with activities that happen according to the laws of Nature. This is like the driver who understands that her car moves according to the nature of the design of its engine and wheels and not because of her own mental chatter. She, the driver, merely activates the car through ignition and points it in the right direction and the car does much of the rest of the work because it is designed that way. Krishna urges Arjuna to view his body and his senses like a car. Although the car might be damaged, he, the driver, is aware that he is not damaged. Krishna makes it clear to Arjuna that his awareness is not what is doing the action; it is the senses through their interaction with their sense objects that are doing the action. Action is caused by the biophysical body in accordance with the laws of nature. The awareness behind the action is like the initial ignition that sets the action in motion. Awareness, like an expert driver, merely *ignites and guides* the action:

> When talking, giving, taking,
>> Opening and closing his eyes,
>> He keeps thinking, "It is the senses
>> That engage in sense objects."

*(5.9)*

Timeless leaders identify with awareness, which is action-less. Therefore, even in the middle of the most intense activity, they remain unattached like a lotus flower that grows in the water and yet is not wet. In this, their actions become more precise and fluent. Most leaders in organizations are evaluated by the quantity of their actions, whereas they should be measured rather by the quality of what they do.

The dictates of a can-do environment prevent the unleashing of this quality of awareness in action. When this awareness is wrongly identified as the agent of action, leaders commit themselves to all kinds of egocentric behaviors that lead them down the wrong path. A driver gets caught by the traffic police for reckless driving because he has momentarily become unaware: His ego has taken possession of the wheel rather than his hands. When leaders move up in the hierarchy of their organization most of their problems turn out to be not technical but behavioral. The source of all behavioral problems that leaders face can be traced back to the *ego*, which conditions and clouds their awareness by giving to it the false notion of being the *doer.* Timeless leadership is the reversal of the journey of the doer. This can be achieved only by the progressive elimination of ego-centered activity and the practice of selfless and dedicated awareness-centered actions.

Leadership becomes timeless when a leader is able to shift from egocentric to awareness-centric action. The ego works within the limits of time and space. Awareness is not limited by time or place.

# SUTRA 6

## LEADERS ARE MASTERS OF THEIR MINDS

## The Art and Practice of Meditation

Krishna teaches Arjuna the wisdom of minding the mind. When the mind of the leader is stuck in Self image, he suffers alienation from his real Self. Arjuna is a victim of such a predicament. He describes to Krishna the elusive and uncontrollable nature of his mind. Krishna acknowledges the problem and shows him the path of taming the unsteady mind by the practice of meditation and dispassion. Krishna sheds light on the three disciplines of the mastery of the mind: concentration, detachment, and transcendence. Finally, he urges Arjuna to experience the power of stillness where the mind withdraws from illusory Self image only to abide in the infinite Self.

## SEPARATING THE SELF IMAGE FROM THE REAL SELF

> One who has conquered his own Self image
>> Has attained to the calm of Self mastery
>> Then, he is established in his Supreme Self that is perfectly poised in cold or heat,
>>> Pleasure or pain, honour or contempt.
>
> *(6.7)*

Krishna's words to Arjuna echo one of the most profound truths of classical Indian wisdom:

> His own self must be conquered by the king for all time; then only are his enemies to be conquered.
> *(Rishi Vyasa,* The Mahabharata, *1000 B.C.)*

Many of our problems are self-created. The source of self-created problems is the fact that we mistake the Self image for our real Self.

*Self image* is a cluster of names and forms by which leaders differentiate themselves from the rest of their environment. They have different Self images as a parent, as a spouse, or as a colleague. They perform various roles in various spheres of life. Each of these roles creates a certain impression of the Self in our consciousness. Thus, one sees oneself as a liberal parent or as a task-oriented boss or as a considerate spouse. All these images temporarily help leaders stabilize their identities in their own eyes.

The problem occurs whenever leaders confront a reality not consistent with their Self image. For instance, when one receives information from the outside world that one is an autocratic boss, or an uncaring spouse, or an "an ugly fat slob," one's Self image is hurt. Leaders attempt to defend their Self image by various means. They may become angry or indifferent to the outside reality. They may take negative feedback from others too seriously and feel dejected. They may also try to conform to something they imagine to be socially acceptable. All these methods may give them a temporary sense of relief, but they keep leaders in the anxious pursuit of the mirage that is their Self image.

Self image makes us vulnerable to changes outside us. If our Self image is one of an evergreen youth, the appearance of the first grey hair makes us lose sleep. We are traumatized by a single rejection slip from an editor if our Self image is that of a successful writer. Our Self image makes us vulnerable simply because much of this image is constantly being threatened by reality. Self image is a frozen model of our real Self. Just as a model is a symbol or attribute of the reality it represents and not the entire reality, one's Self image is merely a projection of the real Self. More often than not, this projection is a distortion of the real Self, just as a shadow is a distortion of the real substance.

Krishna is guiding Arjuna toward the discovery of the real Self. When Arjuna's Self image comes into collision course with his real Self, the image has to yield. Krishna says that Self image has to change in accordance with the real Self. If the leader falls prey to his Self image, his real Self becomes his worst enemy. When he steps out of the shadow of his Self image and into the light of his real Self, the real Self becomes his greatest ally:

> He should elevate himself by the power of the real Self,
>> Not degrade himself;
>> For the self is its own friend
>> And its own worst foe.

> *(6.5)*

How does one go beyond the veil of Self image in search of the real Self? The quest for the Self can begin only when we have turned our attention from the world outside to the world inside. Timeless leaders know that Self image is nothing but the projection of the ego, which is subject to endorsement by the world outside. Thus the ego's position constantly changes in order for it to adjust to the world's opinion. The ego projects many fanciful notions of the real Self. The ego-self is bound by those emotions that make leaders feel insecure and separate: Fear, jealousy, hatred, and false pride are the accompaniments of Self image that the ego tries to defend. Self image is guided primarily by the instinct of psychological survival.

The real Self, however, is unperturbed, for it has nothing to defend. Timeless leaders drop those fanciful Self images created by tags and titles and become identified with their real, unchanging Self. It is then that they begin to access those empowering values of the real Self: compassion, love, freedom, and forgiveness. It is from this Self that a Christ can ask for forgiveness for His murderers. It is from this real Self that Buddha can say, "Hatred does not cease with hatred but with love." It is from this real Self that Krishna can assert, "Arjuna, this real Self can neither kill nor be killed." When leaders are stuck in their behaviours based on fight-or-flight instincts, the real Self is obscured from their view. When they are able to lift themselves from these instincts, they befriend their real Self.

Most of the time leaders are not aware of their real Self because their minds have been burdened with many layers of experiences. An unexamined mind is like a bright mirror that has gathered dust for many years. Such a mind is unable to reflect the light of the real Self. I have often asked leaders from all walks of life, "Who are you?" I receive predictable answers such as, "I am an engineer," or "a marketing manager," or "an ear-nose-throat specialist." The next question I ask is, "Who knows you are all of these?" This time the answers revolve around "mind" or "thought." Then I ask the clincher: "Who knows you have a mind? Have you observed your own mind?" This time a silence descends on my audience, during which leaders begin to reflect on the operations of their own mind.

## MASTERY OF THE MIND

Just as an expert learns to master his craft, a leader learns to master his mind. A leader has to work with many minds. Before he can command others, he has to know how to command his own mental forces. Arjuna, like any of us, feels that the mind is as elusive as it is uncontrollable:

> The mind is restless, O Krishna, turbulent, strong and unyielding;
> It is as difficult to control it as it is to control the wind.
>
> *(6.34)*

Krishna acknowledges that it is not easy for Arjuna to achieve mastery of the mind. But he suggests that it is quite possible to do so:

> Without doubt, the mind
> Is unsteady and hard to hold,
> But practice and dispassion
> Can restrain it, Arjuna.
>
> *(6.35)*

First, Krishna describes the nature of the problem: mind as unsteady and difficult to hold. Second, he gives to Arjuna the solution: The only way to harness the mind is through practice and dispassion. We shall first analyze the problem. To begin with, the mind is nothing but the flow of thought. Such a mind moves tempestuously like a flooding river as thought currents rush through in tumultuous waves. Arjuna describes his mind in three ways:

1. Turbulent because of emotional agitation
2. Strong in its attachment to objects of the senses
3. Unyielding in its movement through the familiar path as it becomes a slave of habit

This is the nature of a mind that is born free but gets burdened by the weight of memories and the structure of past experiences. Such a mind, as Arjuna discovers, finds it very difficult to deal with the unstructured and the unexpected aspects of life. It is very difficult to apply yesterday's solution to today's problem. That's what most leaders try to do and so they fail, because they do not pay enough attention to how their mind functions.

Acknowledging the difficulty in controlling such a mind, Krishna tells Arjuna that the mind can be mastered by practice. This practice involves being a constant observer of the content and movement of the mind. This is simply the art and practice of meditation. An unobserved mind accumulates hidden motives and conditioned thought flow. Most of the mind's energy is spent in holding onto its accumulations and projections. Most leaders hold onto experiences of past successes and project these onto their future. This works if the future is predictably like the past. However, when the future takes a U-turn, such a conditioned mind is caught napping.

To practice observing the limiting structures of one's own mind is to free the mind from the burden of its accumulation. If you did not convert the movement of your thought into a personal psychological possession by identifying yourself with the movement, your mind would cease to be restless and burdensome. When unburdened, the mind is illumined and rendered transparent. Such a mind begins to reflect dispassionately the reality around it just as a clean mirror truthfully reflects the image of reality before it. The mastery of mind is about purity and wholeness of perception: It is the art of being fully present in the moment. Timeless leaders are able to meet the challenges of the future not by going back to their past memories but by being totally present to the reality of the moment.

The practice of meditation results in dispassion. Dispassion creates a space between you and your thought flow. Your perception of thought flow affects and regulates it like a traffic cop regulates the flow of traffic. A dispassionate mind is aware of diversity and differences of forms without getting overtly judgemental about them. Such a mind does not get caught in the external appearance of forms and is capable of seeing the intrinsic value of each form.

> Arming himself with discipline,
> > Seeing everything with an equal eye,
> > He sees the Self in all creatures
> > And all creatures in the Self.

> *(6.29)*

A dispassionate mind is established in serenity. It is a mind poised like the steady light of a lamp that does not flicker because it is a windless day. The steady light of the lamp is a metaphor for a mind that rests in the still, unchanging, and timeless soul Self. A mind that is free of the content of memory begins to see that all thought and indeed all action emerges from the stillness of no-thought and no-action. This happens in the same manner in which the dynamism of a forest emerges from the stillness of a single seed.

Krishna marks out the journey of maturation from the learner to the timeless leader. The learner starts with watchful action. He practices the art of mind watching even in the midst of action until he reaches that tranquil state where the mind is established. When he reaches this state he no longer has to act; all he need do is remain tranquil. Action simply flows from this space of tranquility. This learning process is somewhat like learning to ride a bicycle. One starts by practicing riding with deliberate and vigorous movement of the limbs. When a person matures as a bicyclist, her mind has already developed the knowledge or knack for bicycling. From the core of this knowledge she can bike anytime, even if she stops practicing.

> Action is the means for a learner
> > Who seeks to mature in discipline;
> > Tranquillity is the means
> > For the one who is mature in discipline.

> *(6.3)*

## DISCIPLINES OF MASTERY: CONCENTRATION, DETACHMENT, AND TRANSCENDENCE

Krishna prepares Arjuna for the mastery of the mind by taking him through three steps:

1. Concentration
2. Detachment
3. Transcendence

### *Concentration*

> Firmly hold the body, the head and the neck erect and still.
> Gaze at the tip of the nose without looking around.
>
> *(6.13)*

Concentration is the process through which the leader can access the subtle ability of the mind to remain focussed on an object or a thought for a sustained length of time. Concentration begins with keeping the body in a state of alertness. Unless the body is alert, the mind cannot be concentrated. The head, neck, and backbone are aligned in a straight line and the eyes are focused inward so that visual distractions can be minimised. Concentration happens when the body-mind complex becomes as coherent as a laser beam that unifies the diffused waves of light into one sharp focal point. Krishna describes a fully concentrated mind as "an unflickering lamp set in a windless place."

### *Detachment*

Krishna then describes the art and science of detachment to Arjuna:

> From whatever cause the restless and unsteady mind wanders away, from that let him restrain it, and bring it back under the control of the Self.
>
> *(6.26)*

A mind that is irresolute and unsteady constantly barks like a stray dog at whatever catches its fancy. The ability to restrain the mind from its habitual excursions in the outer world of the senses comes from the power of detachment. Human consciousness is conditioned by repeating the same traffic of thought over and over again. The mental process of worrying happens because of repeated reproduction of thought forms that assume an unconscious momentum. Detachment is the human capacity to be conscious of this autopilot momentum of the mind and to restrain the thought forces from repeating a set pattern. When the intellect is able to hold the mind and its automatic thought movements with a tight leash, the barking mind ceases to wander around. The intellect is like the leash, but what really holds the leash is the soft power of the conscious Self that stands behind the intellect.

## Transcendence

Transcendence is the final step when the mind and its movements are completely interiorized. At this point the body and the mind are united in one state, free from the fluctuations of thought waves. The breathing process becomes calm to the point of stillness as the thought waves subside in the infinite field of consciousness. If thoughts can be compared to waves and consciousness to the deep sea, then transcendence can be experienced as the merger of the individual waves in the vast depths of the sea. Transcendence is the ultimate discipline of the mind. It is the realization of the mind's inherent unity with its conscious source and its environment.

## THE POWER OF STILLNESS

How does one begin the conquest of the turbulent mind? Krishna's prescription is to return to the calm and stillness of the real Self. As we said earlier, Self image is characterized by change and anxiety while the real Self stands still in intense observation. Stillness is strength. Stillness is the power-point behind intense action. The eye of the cyclone is an intense stillness at the center of the storm. Timeless leaders have taught us the art and science of always being still. The Buddha attained enlightenment in stillness. Muhammed sat still in a cave. The Old Testament says, "Be still and know that I am God" (Psalm 46:10).

Nelson Mandela was in prison for nearly three decades. I was curious to know how he lived in a prison for so long. I visited the Robben Island off the coast of Cape Town in South Africa to see the prison in which Mandela had lived for 17 years. It was a tiny room with no toilet, inside a high-walled concrete structure. Mandela, the great revolutionary leader, maintained himself in the stillness of his dignity day after day, year after year. When the prison guards forced all the other prisoners to run, Mandela stood still and walked slowly despite the provocation of his oppressors. The amazing thing is that the prison guards did not torture Mandela into submission; they were compelled to walk behind Mandela at a pace decided by him.

Timeless leaders succeed only by the application of stillness. A mind that is restless, anxious, and nervous always misses the mark. Only a steady, controlled, almost machinelike hand can shoot the arrow that hits the bull's-eye. Krishna speaks of being indivisibly one with one's goal, even like the arrowhead that has stuck into the target. An undivided concentration naturally brings about an absolutely unshakable stillness. This stillness is like a tiger crouching before it pounces on its prey. The prey remains spellbound, unable to run away. The tiger's gaze is fixed upon its goal; it casts a magical spell as it were and its unruffled will prevails over its victim's wish to run away.

The Mother, the spirit consort of Rishi Aurobindo, one of the greatest spiritual leaders of India, tells how the energy of stillness can be achieved and what are the conditions that maintain such energy. She says that the first condition is *self-confidence*. This is nothing but having trust in oneself, the full faith that one is able to do something. A pessimist, a half-hearted doubter, or a defeatist can never achieve anything in this world. All successful people, whatever share they agree to give to chance, always have immense hope and faith. Against failures and against tremendous odds they have always persisted, always believed in their star. Of course, the self-confidence sometimes overrides itself and becomes conceit and arrogance. Then you go beyond your depth, tempt the fates beyond your control, and open the door to failure. So, along with self-confidence, there must be an element of sobriety; we will call it *modesty*—true modesty that can perceive the extreme limits of the possible and the impossible. Such modesty itself is a source of serenity and calmness in the mind and nerves.

Finally, the journey toward Self-realization involves the disciplines of *silence* and *solitude*. Silence frees us from the noise of our externalized consciousness and allows us to probe our inner voice. Solitude enables one to be intimate with oneself. In deep silence and solitude we begin to glimpse the truth of our lives. We realize that whatever exists is an expression of existence and that our many ways of living are expressions of life itself. The *Bhagavad Gita* tells us, "The unreal has no being: the real never ceases to be. The final truth about them both has thus been perceived by the seers of ultimate reality" (2.16).

# LEADERS ARE INTEGRATORS

## The Freedom of "I Am"

### CONTEXT

Krishna reveals himself as the liberator whose primary work is to address human suffering. He tells Arjuna about four kinds of suffering that human beings seek freedom from. Krishna describes the role of the leader as the integrator who brings cessation of suffering by forging unity in a world of conflict. An integrated leader unites a diversity of people and processes like the thread of a necklace that holds many pearls together. He expresses himself in his full glory as the essence and the presence in every form and phenomenon. Krishna thus inspires Arjuna to rise above the three modes of Nature and to the integral knowledge of the Absolute.

## ARJUNA'S JOURNEY FROM IGNORANCE TO WISDOM

Timeless leaders realize that knowledge is required to make a living while wisdom is necessary to live a fully functional and evolving life. Very often one is asked, are leaders born or made? Leaders can be made provided they are born with some inherent qualities of the head and heart such as courage, intelligence, compassion and wisdom. Wisdom is nothing but the realization of who we are and what constitutes our inherent nature.

Knowledge is what we acquire systematically in the classrooms and in our places of work. Therefore knowledge is very useful to get by in the world. But such knowledge becomes useless unless we know ourselves well enough. Take the case of Arjuna. He is a highly skilled archer. He is the stuff that heroes are made of. Yet, with all his knowledge of warfare Arjuna fails to lead himself in the battle field. Arjuna fails because he is ignorant of the living wisdom that comes from the study of one's own Self. This is the difference between Arjuna and Krishna: the difference between ignorance and wisdom.

In his ignorance Arjuna's thinks that human life is no more than the combination of eight elements: earth, water, air, fire, space, mind, intellect and ego. These constitute the body-mind-senses complex that Arjuna identifies as his own self. Krishna teaches him that there is much more to life than these eight elements:

> My nature has eight aspects:
>     Earth, water, fire, wind, space,
>     Mind, understanding, and individuality.
>     This is my lower nature.
>     Know my higher nature, too,

The life-force
That sustains this universe.

*(7.4/7.5)*

These eight elements are guided by a higher life force: the human spirit. Krishna is the embodiment of this spirit.

A timeless leader like Krishna recognizes the supremacy of spirit over the matter. This is true of everyday life as well as organizational life. For instance, consider *team spirit*, which we often use to describe excellent teamwork in organizations. This spirit is nothing but the shared life force that connects and transcends the physical-mental complex of the individual team members.

Krishna thus reveals to Arjuna the timeless secret of excellence: Look for the essential life giving spirit in all of mundane nature. Krishna says to Arjuna in a poetic rapture:

I am the taste of water and the light in the moon and the Sun.
I am the silent spirit of sound and the manliness in man.
I am the fragrance of the earth and the brilliance of a fire ablaze.
I am the life in all beings and the austerity of a sage.
I am the eternal seed of all beings and from me all of Nature arises.
I am the splendour of all that is splendid and the wisdom of the wise.

*(7.8)*

This, then, is the journey of "I am" from the mundane body-mind-senses complex to the very essence of life. Arjuna's consciousness is stuck in the eight elements of his mundane nature. Krishna leaves Arjuna momentarily unstuck, freeing him from his self-created ignorance. Arjuna lives in a very small illusory world. He cannot conceive of the vast potential that lies within him. Krishna presents to Arjuna a vision of life beyond the ordinary. In this Krishna leads Arjuna from darkness to light.

## TIMELESS LEADERS INTEGRATE PEOPLE AND PROCESSES

One of the fundamental tasks of leadership is the task of integration. Leaders do not take sides in the case of a conflict; they often bring the two sides together. Leaders integrate the world of diversity and differences into a unity of purpose. Leadership is the search for synergy, symphony, and symmetry in a world of conflict and disorder.

Krishna uses a striking metaphor to explain this role of the timeless leader to Arjuna:

> O Arjuna, everything is held together by me like a necklace
> of pearls on a string.
>
> *(7.7)*

The pearls in the necklace represent the diversity of people in an organization. Like people, these pearls come in different shapes and sizes and colours. The unseen thread holding the pearls together is the integrating life force of the leader. The pearls represent the body-mind-senses complex while the leader represents the unifying spirit that ties many such complex human beings into a whole and harmonious system.

Krishna is drawing Arjuna's attention to the reality of systemic intelligence, which renders complex organizational processes into a coherent whole. This intelligence is like the ignition of a car, which sets the different parts of the car into well-coordinated movement. Without this ignition, the car would remain a static structure without its inherent dynamism.

From where does the leader derive the power of integration? What is the source of a leader's ability to connect people to a common cause? What is that discipline that enables a leader to attract people to such a cause? Krishna invites Arjuna to undertake the timeless journey of leaders: the journey toward an integral being. Integral beings become conscious of a life of oneness with themselves and their universe. They act from the wholeness of this consciousness. In actual behavior they demonstrate a harmony and unique synchronicity between their beliefs and their actions. Their body-mind-senses complex orchestrates itself to the effortless rhythms of the universe.

Krishna emphatically tells Arjuna: "Everything depends on me, as pearls on a thread." Krishna is pointing toward the integrating power of the universe as it works through the being of a timeless leader. What is that power that holds all planets in their orbits? What is it that creates the symphony of the stars? Everything in the universe depends on this unifying and integrating principle that Krishna embodies.

An integral leader begins to experience spiritual affinity with the natural order of the universe; his inner nature becomes one with outer Nature. Leaders with integrity attract followers spontaneously, even beyond their lifetimes. For such leaders life becomes one song—a universe—of thought, feeling, and action. *Integrity* is another expression for this one song. Integrity is more than just socially sanctioned, conditioned behavior. It is a spontaneous life force that connects all our life's experiences in a unique wholeness—like the string in the necklace that holds the pearls together.

## THE LEADER'S WORLD: A REFLECTION OF UNMANIFEST *DHARMA*

*Dharma* is the integral and living principle that works through us. To act according to our *dharma* is to act righteously in accordance with this integrating principle. How does the leader know that there is such an integrating principle? Imagine that you have a glass prism that scatters light into seven different colours: violet, indigo, blue, green, yellow, orange, and red. We can see these seven colours distinctly with the naked eye. Yet, the pure light from which these colours have emerged remains invisible to us. We can see the colours emerging from this light, yet we can't see the light itself.

*Dharma* works through us like the invisible light that manifests itself in many colours. In human nature, *dharma* manifests in three psychological forces: inertia, dynamism, and illumination. These are the three forces that reveal themselves through the colourful kaleidoscope of human nature. Behind these forces is the invisible light of unmanifest *dharma*. Krishna explains this principle to Arjuna:

> Know that Nature's qualities
> > Come from me—lucidity,
> > Passion, and dark inertia;
> > I am not in them; they are in me.
>
> *(7.12)*

In the human form everyone can experience the manifestation of our *dharma* in the three observable states: inertia, dynamism, and illumination. It is one *dharma* of human consciousness manifesting in three different states. When we are asleep we are in the grip of inertia. Our body's movement is restricted in this sleep state. When we wake up we are propelled by the force of dynamism that leads us to activity. But when illumination prevails we become reflective and peaceful. These states are three different modifications of one unbroken consciousness, just as ice, fluid, and steam are three different modifications of one unmanifest *dharma* of water. We can't see the *dharma* of water with the naked eye, yet we know that such a *dharma* exists as an unalterable and universal law of water (a compound combining two parts hydrogen and one part oxygen). We cannot see the "wetness" of water, yet we know it when we get wet that we are in contact with water.

Just as all the different qualities of water come from its basic *dharma*, all qualities of human nature come from one unmanifest source. Krishna explains to Arjuna that He is that source. Krishna is the unmanifest spirit that is hidden behind our waking, sleeping, and dreaming states. He says,

> I am not in them; they are in me.

Quite simply, *dharma* is inaccessible through our sensory modes of perception in the sleeping, dreaming, or wakeful states. Neither can *dharma* be merely spoken about, as it manifests in deeds and not in words. In reality, *dharma* has to be lived. Water does not announce its basic *dharma* of wetness: It just acts out its *dharma* by wetting whoever comes in direct contact with it. Those leaders who live *dharma* rather than just speak about it understand that the power of *dharma* comes only when you practice it.

How does a leader act out his *dharma* in the world if he can't see it? One way to act out one's *dharma* is through righteous action. Arjuna represents the minority of five Pandavas in the war against the mighty majority of the Kauravas. Yet, Arjuna's strength comes from the *dharma* of the righteous war that he is fighting. Arjuna is fighting for a just cause. Action has no power in itself. It draws its power from the unmanifest purpose or *dharma* behind it. That's why action backed by the right cause is important. A leader's action bears the signature of the justness of a great cause.

## FROM EGO-CENTERED TO SPIRIT-CENTERED LEADERSHIP

The ego is like a tragic hero. It is delusional. A leader caught in the whirlpool of the ego fails to see a world beyond power, privilege, and petty perquisites that come from occupying a position. An egocentric leader experiences the feelings of victor or victim. When success comes, such leaders act like the victor. When failure stares them in the face, they hide behind the façade of the victim. Such is Arjuna's plight. Krishna is intent on removing the veil created by the ego. He tells Arjuna:

> All this universe, deluded
>> By the qualities inherent in Nature,
>> Fails to know that I am
>> Beyond them and unchanging.

*(7.13)*

When he says "I am," Krishna refers to the spirit center from where he can clearly see through the delusions of his protégé Arjuna. How is this delusion created in Arjuna's mind? Imagine a person who is being driven over a frozen lake on a cold winter day. This man has lived all his life in a tropical country and has never seen snow before. If his driver were to tell him that they were driving across a frozen lake, the man from the tropics would find it difficult to believe. Since he has never seen a lake freeze into solid ice, his ego will refuse to accept that one can really drive over a vast body of frozen water. But the driver, who is a native of the cold country, would find nothing strange about this as he is used to this kind of driving. Krishna, the charioteer, is like that driver trying to explain to Arjuna the reality of the situation. Krishna is conscious of the spirit center. From this center a leader can discriminate between what is real and what is illusion.

Very often, egocentric leaders fail to recognize the real intent of the people they are leading. They get caught in the trap of flattery and suspect the motives of those with dissenting views. When established in the spirit center a timeless leader begins to develop greater empathy and insight into human nature. Timeless leaders are quick to discover the unchanging core of spirit that is the deepest and highest human aspiration. Like Krishna, these leaders are able to lead their people to this very core. This is the ultimate goal of timeless leadership: to lead people to their essential spiritual selves.

# LEADERS LIBERATE THEMSELVES AND OTHERS FROM SUFFERING

> Four kinds of virtuous men seek me, Arjuna:
>> The distressed; the desirous, the inquisitive,
>> And those in search of the knowledge of the absolute.
>
>> *(7.16)*

Krishna tells Arjuna that there are four categories of followers or devotees that are attracted to him:

1. Those in distress
2. Those looking for fulfilment of their personal desires
3. Those yearning for knowledge
4. Those seeking wisdom

Krishna teaches Arjuna what leaders are supposed to do: They liberate themselves and others from suffering. He elaborates four different kinds of suffering that we face in the human condition. The first kind is that of *physical pain and mental distress*. People in the world suffer not just the pangs of hunger and poverty but also the mental distress caused by labels and designations. In many organizations people suffer because of the way they are categorized by the organization. A manager may find himself boxed inside a particular role and condemned to hours of drudgery. There is suffering when relationships within organizations become hostile and stressful due to performance pressures.

The second kind of suffering happens because of *unfulfilled desires*. Most people in organizations think of fulfilment only in terms of the next promotion or the next big bonus, the next vacation or the next car. This kind of fulfilment, even if we achieve our objects of desire, turns out to be as deceptive as a mirage that falsely promises water in a desert. It merely helps us shift the burden of our desirous and anxious minds from one thing to another. Our dependence on the people who could grant our desires keeps mounting. We keep thinking that ultimate success lies just around the corner. However, true fulfilment comes from what Krishna describes as "equanimity of mind." This is a state of mind that is neither disproportionately elated in possessing the object of desire nor too depressed when we are dispossessed of what we hold as ours. A leader like Krishna leads us to this space of Self-realization wherein we find the completion of all our desires and cessation of all our anxieties.

The third kind of suffering happens when we do not have the right *knowledge* about who we are. This is suffering that comes from identity crisis. We have merely a casual curiosity about who we are beyond our physical body. We fail to recognize that although we have a body we are not the body; we have a mind but we are not the mind. This kind of suffering comes from forgetfulness of our essential Self. Imagine what would happen if the owner of a large business empire suddenly loses his memory, gets lost in a busy metropolis, and begins to beg for a living. Unless he retrieves his memory or unless some of his friends remind him of his real status he will continue to suffer the lot of a beggar because he does not have the right knowledge of who he is.

Krishna talks about the fourth kind of followers, who are among the best and the rarest. They do not make too many demands, nor do they expect material rewards. They have already reached a state of Self-actualization. They are not interested so much in fulfilment of their personal ambition as in living for a cause greater than themselves. These followers are the *seekers of wisdom*. Their desires are not contrary to their essential *dharma*. Their only wish is to discover another dimension of life beyond their ego. Krishna says that these are the wise ones who offer themselves with all their personal ambitions as a sacrifice to a life of service. If they suffer, it is because of their yearning for their true Self.

The common feature of all these categories of followers is that all of them wish to end their suffering. However, their suffering comes from different planes of consciousness. Therefore, they need to be addressed differently. Someone who suffers financially is unlikely to heed the message of Self-realization. Similarly, one who is already Self-actualized is unlikely to be motivated by more money than he requires. Thus Krishna establishes the timeless yearning of the human condition to bring an end to suffering. It is the leader's unique privilege to be able to liberate others from their self-created delusions. True leaders realize that there is no such thing as a merely personal salvation. Liberation is a *shared* experience. In a living organization, unless the lowest in the hierarchy can be whatever he or she wants to be, the highest in the hierarchy cannot be what he or she wishes to be. Such is the interdependent nature of the human condition.

Krishna is a timeless leader because he not only has keen insight into the nature of human motivation but also has a way out of human suffering, which is perennial.

# SUTRA 8

# TIMELESS LEADERSHIP

## Decoding the Meaning of Life

Arjuna's real questions to Krishna are about the meaning of life. He asks:

- What does it mean to be a timeless leader?
- How does such a leader's work evolve through the cycle of life?

Krishna clearly carves out the path of evolution of the timeless leader. He also elaborates on the relationship between the imperishable being and the perishable world of thoughts and emotions. He helps Arjuna understand the ultimate reality of leadership in all its facets: the objective as well as the subjective; the universal as well as the personal. He brings home to Arjuna that the cycle of evolution of form and phenomena is contained in one unchanging reality of being that he describes as *Brahma*.

## TIMELESS LEADERS EXPLORE THE ULTIMATE MEANING OF LIFE

Can the business of business and the business of life be any different? Life asks what we must live for and not just what we have to live by. If business becomes merely the means of living, then it loses meaning for us. Work becomes a chore—a means of making a living at the expense of the meaning of life. Such a business eventually becomes demeaning. The real question we must ask while we are in business is: What is the meaning of this work for me? If we find an answer to this question, the business of business and the business of life become one and the same: What are we living and working for? Arjuna asks the same question to Krishna—what is the meaning of this life? What are we fighting and living for?

Krishna responds to Arjuna by saying that the meaning of life can be found only when we learn to explore the ultimate source of our life and our work. To do this we must break through the physical and mental motivators of life, which are perishable, and access the higher dimension of energy of *being*, which is imperishable. The imperishable being that Krishna describes as Brahma is the very source of our life and work. Krishna transports Arjuna from the mundane plane of existence, in which body and mind seem like the apparent source of energy, to a higher realm. Krishna traces all work and all business to the imperishable being as the real source. He says that this source is Brahma:

> Brahma is the imperishable Supreme; His essential Nature is Self Knowledge. The creative capacity that causes all forms and phenomena is called Work.
>
> *(8.3)*

In an organization, what we typically mean by *work* is nothing more than physical or mental effort. However, Krishna is taking Arjuna much deeper in his search for meaning in work. He advises Arjuna not to be attached to the body or get tied down to his mind in his search for the ultimate source of work. He says work will become truly meaningful when we learn to dedicate ourselves to the ultimate life quest: the search for our being. He urges Arjuna to dedicate all his physical and mental energy to the search for this imperishable being even as he works with perishable forms and phenomena.

In our ordinary state of mind we see our imperishable being in a very distorted form, through the mirrors of our body and our mind. When we see our imperishable being reflected in this way, we get an incorrect picture of the meaning of our life and work.

## THE MULTIDIMENSIONAL MEANING OF LIFE

Life is a dynamic dance of energies. These energies are organized in multidimensional layers. The universe of appearances in the outer world, as well the inner subjective world of thoughts, emotions, and perceptions, are contained within the larger womb of Brahma, which is the ultimate Reality. Arjuna asks:

> What is Brahma the Absolute? What is the Self and what is that work that helps one evolve? How does one know the ultimate Reality in the course of evolution?
>
> *(8.1–2)*

Krishna explains to Arjuna the multidimensional organization of life. The first dimension of life is our objective world, which is governed by the elements. This is the world of the physical nature of objects and events that we all can touch, taste, see, hear, and feel. Krishna describes this as *Adhibhuta*. Second, there is the inner psychological world of experiences known as *Adhiyagna*. This is the world of thoughts and emotions—human actions and interactions. Third, the ultimate governing principle of *Adhidaiva*. This principle is like a transcendental being who regulates the relationship between the physical and psychological world without being part of either. This is the world of the imperishable being working as the observer. This being is our cosmic supervisor that synchronizes the harmonious working of the entire universe.

Arjuna's next question is, "How does one evolve through work to realize the ultimate reality?" Krishna suggests to Arjuna that to realize the ultimate reality one has to undertake the heroic journey toward perfect understanding, selfless work, and unswerving devotion to the supreme reality. What is perfect understanding? It is the same as the search for the ultimate meaning of life. The meaning of life is clouded by an array of thoughts and motives that do not allow us to see our ultimate reality. These thoughts are like barriers that a cloudy sky puts up between us and the Sun. To know the imperishable reality, the leader must learn to convert the energy of thought into the energy of understanding. While thought results in neural noise, true understanding happens when this noise dissolves in the depth of silence. This silent awareness behind thoughts is "Brahma"—the imperishable source of creation. All that is enduring in the world of art, music, science, and commerce comes from this space of silence that is Brahma.

Such a perfect understanding of our reality goes hand in hand with unselfish work. Why is that so? Our ultimate reality is that we are Brahma—the imperishable being. Our apparent reality is that we are a combination of the objective world and the subjective self. When our work is tied to the selfish motive of gaining advantages for ourselves we lose the perfect understanding of our real nature and succumb to our apparent reality. When you put a fence around human beings you get sheep. The fence of selfish work makes us prisoners of our

herd instinct. Krishna leads Arjuna from the darkness of ignorance of his ultimate reality. He says:

> Conceive the Supreme person as Omniscient and the Ancient
> Ruler of this universe; One who is smaller than an atom yet
> the One who is Omnipresent. This person is effulgent like the
> Sun that transports you beyond the darkness of ignorance.
>
> *(8.9)*

## CREATION IS SACRIFICING
## THE SMALLER FOR THE SAKE
## OF THE GREATER

How can someone who is smaller than an atom be the
Omniscient Creator at the same time? Krishna unravels this
paradox by explaining to Arjuna that creation is an ongoing
process of sacrificing the smaller for the greater. When we split
an atom to explore the latent energies within its nucleus we
open the doors to greater and *subtler* energy. A nuclear explosion has the potency to engulf an entire city with its energy.
When an atom breaks open and sacrifices its form it can be the
source of great dynamism. There is an order and organization
of energy within an atom *from the gross to the subtle.* The gross
has to be sacrificed and split open for the subtle energy to
emerge. Krishna explains that our life, on the contrary, is an
organization of energies moving from the higher to the lower;
from the macrocosm to the microcosm; *from the subtle to the
gross.* A leader must understand the science of life and live
according to this organizing principle of life: the subtle and
higher energy drives the gross and lower energy.

The core message of the science of life is that by sacrificing
the smaller and the lower, we reclaim the greater and the
higher. As in the physical universe, a leader must learn to sacrifice lower ambition for higher aspiration. Very often ambition

uses up life's energy in compulsive behaviour, such as addiction to more money, power, or fame. Leaders caught in the trap of ambition become vulnerable to flattery by their subordinates. They squander energy by being too possessive about their position and power. Ambitious leaders often use people as steppingstones up to their own pedestals. Ambition binds them to lower-order emotions such as fear, jealousy, and possessiveness. The arc of ambition takes us upward in a misleading curve and then brings us down with a thud.

Sometimes lower-order ambitions have to be sacrificed for higher-order aspiration. Aspiration makes leaders dream of a better organization, country, or world. In our psychological universe aspiration creates greater energy than ambition does. Ambition is gross; aspiration is subtle. The most successful leaders of this world, such as Buddha, Christ, or Gandhi, gave up personal ambition for a higher aspiration. They created a nuclear explosion of consciousness that continues to influence the world of our thoughts and actions today.

Imagine the leader of an organization who one day decides to sacrifice a career for a calling—what is he likely to get as a result? One such leader, who abandoned the pursuit of a formal degree and made Apple one of the world's greatest brands, said that he dropped out of college and dropped into the larger world of creation.

## THE REAL MEANING OF LIFE IS CONTAINED IN LIFE ITSELF

One of the world's best companies to work for in the field of medical equipment describes its rationale for existence in few simple words: "To restore people to their whole lives." This is the real work of timeless leaders—to restore people to the wholeness of their Being. The real meaning of life is contained in just being the whole of who we are. What are those attributes of being that together give meaning to life? Being has three attributes:

1. *Truth*, which gives meaning to our existence
2. *Consciousness*, which gives meaning to our experiences
3. *Bliss*, which gives meaning to our actions in the pursuit of happiness

Truth is that aspect of our being that is right and secure in itself. Truth does not need the support of anything outside of itself. Truth is Self-referral. This means that truth exists in reference to itself. When a timeless leader relentlessly pursues the path of truth, she is able to realize that all that she needs to know already exists in herself. Truthfulness makes a leader spontaneous, like a flowing river or a blazing fire. Such a leader is not caught in the mind's dogma or prejudices. Indeed, truth is liberating—it liberates both the leader and the follower.

If truth gives meaning to our existence, consciousness gives meaning to all our experiences. Consciousness is not the knowledge that we learn from books or in school. Consciousness is the knowledge that we become. When we are conscious of salt, our whole being experiences what it means to be salty. When a leader is fully conscious he steers clear of secondhand knowledge and third-party opinions and makes decisions from the authenticity of his being. In this, a leader is like a bird that takes flight in an open sky without any outside direction. The bird dares to do this as it is rooted firmly in its internal navigation system. When a leader is similarly rooted in his consciousness he can connect all his experiences to the coherence of this consciousness. This consciousness is the leader's navigation system to take on the uncertainties of the outer world.

Bliss is what we all seek in the garb of pursuit of happiness. Very often the pursuit of happiness leads us to objects, events, and relationships outside ourselves. Yet all our pursuits of happiness in experiences outside ourselves come from the core of bliss, which is our real, intrinsic nature. As philosopher Arthur Schopenhauer once said, it is difficult to find happiness within oneself, but it is impossible to find it anywhere else! A timeless leader, despite all his materialistic hunger, places immense value on the intrinsic nature of happiness. However difficult the journey, the source of happiness has to be found inside. Timeless leaders lead people to their inner source of happiness rather than to external rewards.

## MEANINGFUL WORK: A SYNTHESIS OF REFLECTION AND ACTION

One fundamental role of a leader is the ability to see patterns and detect relationships between events and activities within and outside the organization. In this role a leader is a pattern seeker and a meaning maker. The greatest asset to a leader as he seeks to control the variables that confront him in a globalized world is his *flexibility of mind*. A leader needs an open mind that is not conditioned by repetitive thought and predictable action. Such a mind will be capable of making sense of fast-paced socioeconomic changes that affect his organization. The opposite of an open mind is a closed mind, in which thinking and action are limited to the immediate local and temporal condition. A leader with such a closed mind is bound to fall prey to myopic decision making and short-term activities that will ruin the organization in the long term.

An open mind combines reflection with action. Reflection gives meaning to our actions. In narrating the multidimensional meaning of life, Krishna is enlarging Arjuna's perspective on his life and the work at hand. He is asking Arjuna to see that his immediate work is connected to the ultimate reality of Brahma. Krishna persuades Arjuna that the battle at hand is but a minor ripple in the cosmic pattern of creation. He says that all that we do in the human plane is nothing but a projection of the cosmic work that connects the unmanifest with the manifest. A timeless leader like Krishna can connect his thoughts, emotions, and actions with the supreme pattern of creation represented by Brahma. Reflection is the means through which this connection is made. The more such a connection is established, the more a leader becomes a flawless instrument of the supreme reality or Brahma.

Timeless leaders like Krishna solve problems by placing them in the wider context. When we widen the context the problem gets resolved at its source. Think of a physical ailment that your physician has detected in you. When you first hear of it, it seems like a huge problem. The disease and the pain are experienced in the body, but the problem is a conceptualization of the mind. However, when you discover that a large percentage of the population has the same disease, the problem seems much less acute and therefore much more bearable.

What did you do to solve your problem of a disease that you imagined only you had? All you did was widen the context of the problem, wherein you found that a lot of other people suffered the same disease. This widening of the context helped your mind reprogram an acute problem into a manageable one.

Arjuna sees the work of going into battle as a huge problem. His mind conjectures all kinds of dreadful possibilities. What Krishna does is no more than open up the mind of Arjuna to the larger context of work. He explains that Arjuna's work is more than the physical action experienced by the movements of his body. The physical movements of the body are caused by the movements in the mind. The mind channels its movement to the body through the nervous system. When Arjuna's mind begins to reflect on the broader dimension of work, which Krishna traces back to a cosmic source or Brahma, Arjuna becomes more tranquil. Arjuna begins to see the problem of going to war with a more settled and resolute mind.

Most of our work in our organizations is reflexive (like a kneejerk reaction) rather than reflective. When leaders engage in reflexive action the context of their work is narrowed down to habitual patterns and meaningless chores. Sooner or later such work becomes tedious and wears us out. Timeless leaders like Krishna rescue us from the mental rut and bring us into the infinite cosmic source from which our work derives deep meaning and significance. Krishna thus enables us to synthesise reflection and action in pursuit of work. Such work becomes truly evolutionary.

# SUTRA 9

# THE SOVEREIGN SECRET

## Timeless Leaders Live in a Self-Organizing Universe

In this sutra Krishna shares with Arjuna the sovereign secret of the leader's universe. He calls it a royal secret as it is the basis on which the leader's world is organized. He urges Arjuna to expand his consciousness so that he can see the unity and order of a Self-organizing principle that sustains this world of appearances. Arjuna is advised to shift from his ego as the monitor of all experiences to the transcendental intelligence of the Self that illuminates all experiences. With this expanded consciousness the leader no longer sees himself in the world. Rather, he sees the world in himself. Krishna argues, "I exist unmanifest, throughout the whole universe. Although I don't live in them, all beings live in me." A timeless leader, Krishna resides in the organization of form and phenomena as an unseen intelligence that both includes and transcends the structure of the organization.

## SOVEREIGN SELF AND
## THE PATH OF UNITY

The real presence of a leader is often determined by his absence. The value of a leader in an organization can be experienced in the unseen dimension of intelligence that he leaves behind when he is not there. What is this unseen dimension of intelligence? A cube of ice is dropped into a glass of water. The ice gradually melts away, cooling the water. Even though the *form* of ice is absent inside the glass of water, the ice *functions* in absentia in the coolness of the water. Similarly, a leader who understands the function of the sovereign Self is capable of leading even though he may be absent in form. Krishna tells Arjuna how the gross and visible form of a leader can function invisibly. Krishna compares the leader to that unseen space of intelligence in which organizational processes function like the blowing of the wind:

> Just as the mighty wind, sweeping across the land, rests forever in space,
>> Know that all beings, going through the cycles of life and death, always rest in me.
>> The subtle is all pervasive and always contains the gross.
>
> *(9.6)*

The subtle principle that Krishna refers to here is the sovereign Self that binds different elements of a leader's universe in the unity of intelligence. No organization, whether natural, commercial, or social, can function without this unity of intelligence. Very often leaders end up being the symbol of unity of their organizations. Behind the symbolic presence of the leader, however, the principle of unity works. People choose to cooperate in an organization not because of the formal authority of a leader but because of the desire to be united with an entity that is bigger than themselves.

The functioning of the human body is a great example of the principle of unity. The trillion cells in the body work toward a united goal: preserving the wholeness of the body. When even a single cell is injured the body's entire immune system is activated to serve that single cell. Like any organization that is divided into departments, the overall functioning of the body is distributed in different organs. These organs, such as the brain, heart, lungs, and kidneys, apparently have independent functions. The distribution of the body's energy into separate organs creates the illusion of independence. Yet the energies of all these organs are unified in a web of intelligence. This is why the body feels like one whole organism.

Krishna advises Arjuna to strive for this unity of intelligence by devoting the sum total of his physical and mental energies to that sovereign Self that Krishna represents. He urges Arjuna:

> Fix your mind on Me, be devoted to Me and unite your whole Self with Me.
>
> *(9.34)*

The clarion call of Krishna to Arjuna is not for blind obedience but for enlightened harmonization of the physical, mental, and emotional energies in order to serve the sovereign Self that Krishna refers to as "Me." This "Me" is not the physical body of Krishna but that supreme intelligence or the Self that connects all of us inside our human core. This natural intelligence, though dispersed and diversified in many forms, ultimately leads back to its own source. A leader who is able to devote himself to the pursuit of this intelligence discovers the capacity for Self-rule.

## THE GOVERNANCE OF THE EGO: THE PATH OF DISINTEGRATION

If leaders do not follow the path of Self-organization and Self-rule, then they spiral down the path of ego-based destruction.

Very often the mental energies of a leader assume a controlling monitor called the *ego*. This ego-consciousness tries to assume the role of the sovereign Self. The root cause of the dictatorial leadership of Hitler is that his need for control was so excessive and all-consuming that he took a whole mass of people toward annihilation.

The governance of the ego breeds the need to grasp rather than to give. The tyrants that ruled the world over the ages were all obsessed with personal acquisition at the expense of the common good. The prime reason for the financial melt-down and the consequent global economic crisis can be attributed to the governance of the greedy ego. This, too, is a timeless truth. Our physical structures and mental frames have long received training in getting rather than giving. The ego is the central organizing principle around which we grab and clutch onto experiences that bring us fleeting pleasures and momentary sensations.

Leaders who are governed by their egos are caught in the web of illusions that they themselves spin. These are illusions of grandeur, glamour, fame, and fortune. Jeffrey Keith ("Jeff") Skilling, chief operating officer of the giant energy company, Enron, went to jail for corporate malpractice that resulted in Enron's annihilation. Governed by his ego, Skilling was full of swagger and very often his tactless comments misled his followers. Eventually, Skilling recognized that he had lost his capacity for Self rule. When he was put in prison Skilling stated that the worst witness against him was himself.

Even the legendary Jack Welch was known at the start of his career at General Electric to be arrogant and excessively proud of his talent. However, he did have a midcourse correction from Ego's governance to Self rule when he stated that he was too full of himself. He also realized that there was only a razor's edge between self-confidence and arrogance. The journey from ego's domain to that of the sovereign Self involves walking the razor's edge of awareness of one's own hidden motives and well-disguised intentions.

The Governance of the Ego has as its Board of Directors those precise emotions that Arjuna is familiar with: guilt, fear, pride, shame, and self-pity. Krishna is deftly guiding Arjuna away from the ego's anchors to another plane of awareness where the sovereign Self rules. When Krishna exhorts Arjuna, "Devote yourself! Offer yourself to me," he is asking Arjuna to sacrifice his egocentric thoughts so that he can devote all his energies to discovering the Self that rules the universe. The leader who is governed by the Self sees that it is the Self and not the ego's schemes that drive every thought, every action from the faintest fluttering of the eyelids to the mammoth movement of planets. This realization alone liberates him from the path of erroneous judgments and ineffectual actions.

## SELF-ORGANIZATION: WHEN ORGANIZATION BECOMES COMMUNITY

Before the birth and flourishing of industrial organizations over the past few centuries, the most powerful forms of organization were communities. These communities were religious, social, or cultural groups that shared common interests. Unlike contemporary organizations, however, these communities were driven not by shareholder value or profits, but by a common purpose. The relationship among members of a community was both horizontal and vertical. The horizontal relationship was based on the tasks and roles that the community members performed. The vertical relationship was in the communities' commitment to an ideal or a cause. This ideal was expressed in serving God or the community spirit or a transcendental reality that was greater than the sum total of the members of the community.

Communities were far more integrated psychologically with their organizations because of this vertical relationship to an ideal. In today's corporations, horizontal relationships are expressed by well-defined roles and team orientation to the tasks at hand. However, the vertical relationship that consists in searching for a common spirit or purpose has almost disappeared from the agenda of modern organizations. The result has been the reduction of work to a mundane economic goal and the growing disenchantment of people with what they do in their workplaces and offices.

Arjuna is not a loser; he is simply lost. He cannot see the vertical connection between his work on the battlefield and the greater cause for which he is fighting the battle. Krishna comes to his rescue, however, as he tells Arjuna: You get involved in the battle and leave the worrying to me! Krishna says to Arjuna:

> Let me take the responsibility of your well being.
>> I will take care of your needs.
>> You do the best you can and leave the rest to Me.
>>> *(9.22)*

Krishna is offering a psychologically robust approach to solving the problem of the worrier, Arjuna, so that he can become the true warrior. What exhausts us at work is not the work itself but the worry and anxiety that we associate with our work. These cause psychological wear and tear and drain our energy. Our horizontal relationships produce friction in the form of role conflict and lack of role clarity. In the absence of a vertical relationship with an ideal to which can offer both our failures and our successes, we become emotional wrecks.

What binds a corporation and a community together is timeless leadership. The issue of leadership was as much a concern in traditional communities as it is in contemporary corporations. The traditional Buddhist communities share this common prayer:

> Buddham sharanam gacchami
> Dharmam sharanam gacchami
> Sangham sharanam gacchami

The first line translates as "I remember the Buddha and affirm my commitment to Him." The second line means, "I remember and affirm my allegiance to the principle of *dharma* of which Buddha is the embodiment." The third line says, "I affirm my allegiance to the organization, or *sangha*, which is the community that is devoted to the *dharma* of the Buddha." We see a clear prioritisation of commitments in the members of the Buddhist communities.

The first of these commitments is to the leader (Buddha). The leader is an embodiment of the guiding principle of the organization (*dharma*) as well as the guiding structure (*sangha*). In the leader, the traditional communities saw the ultimate purpose of their lives. The Buddha for them was not so much an individual as he was an embodiment of truth and compassion. The leader's connection with the followers in the community was principle centered. As long as followers were committed to their *dharma* or the right principles they were equal in the eyes of the leader. Krishna says to Arjuna:

> I know no partiality, no bias or prejudice.
>
> *(9.29)*

> Man or woman, king or slave, I see with an equal eye.
>
> *(9.32)*

An organization achieves both horizontal and vertical unity through a community. However, the horizontal relationships between members derive their value from a vertical relationship with the leader. The leader is therefore vested with the responsibility not only of leading the organization but also of being completely integrated with the principles on which the organization is founded. The relationship between the leader and the organization is not contractual but rather integral. In the context of communities, leaders like Krishna lead only because they are totally integrated with the vision of the organization.

Timeless leaders hold communities together on the basis of trust. While leading an Indian community of several million people toward independence, Gandhi based his leadership principle on the notion of the *trusteeship*. This principle came from Gandhi's understanding of the leadership role as that of the trustee responsible for keeping in trust the power given to him by his followers. Trusteeship acknowledges that leaders' power, position, and influence come to them because of the trust that their followers have in them and the principles that the leader lives by. Therefore, timeless leaders are responsible for using their positions, not for personal interest but in the interest of the larger community that has embraced them as leaders.

## THE LAW OF GIVING: BEING AND BECOMING

Timeless leaders are defined not so much by what they do but by who they are. The *being* of a leader is the most critical factor in determining what the leader and his organization become in the ultimate analysis. Krishna has conveyed to Arjuna that his being dwells in the infinite and the timeless. This being, however, functions in the finite space and specific time when He becomes something. This is the essence of the timeless leader's journey: The whole being functions as the part without ever losing the essence of the whole. The light of the Sun is reflected through a prism. The being of white light becomes seven different colours as it passes through the prism. The same white light functions as differentiated colours, yet the original white light remains pure and unsullied by this fragmentation. Krishna says:

> The entire universe has the essence of my unmanifest and timeless being.
>     Although I do not exist physically in all creatures, yet all creatures exist within me.
>
> *(9.4)*

This is similar to the white light that is not visible in all the colours of the spectrum, whereas all the colours can be seen as parts of white light. To take another example, the Sun exists millions of miles away from us. Yet we can take a magnifying glass and burn a piece of paper with the rays of the Sun. The Sun is not physically inside the burning paper, yet it becomes the heat that manifests in the objective phenomenon of the burning paper.

How is it that the timeless being of Krishna is part of our physical world and yet not of it? The reason is simple: Our physical energies are limited by the form of our body; our mental energies are limited by our conditioned mind and our habitual thoughts. But the energy of the unmanifest and timeless being includes and transcends our physical structures and mental formations. It is as difficult to grasp this unmanifest being through our senses as it is to be able to see one's own face without a mirror! Yet, Krishna urges Arjuna to be acquainted with that faceless-face that is nothing but pure and unmanifest being. There is a Zen saying: "What was your face like before you were born?" This is exactly what Krishna is asking Arjuna to consider.

This give-and-take between being and becoming, between the unmanifest and the manifest, is the very basis of our

Self-organizing universe. Everything in our universe follows the law and logic of an open system. An open system continuously exchanges energy with the environment outside its physical boundaries. A seed is an open system that imports energy from soils, Sun, and water. Like a seed that gives up its form to become a tree, an open system surrenders its form to reorganize itself into newer and higher forms. By remaining receptive to new information and by breaking out of its conditioning, an open system, like a seed, is able to access the timeless cycle of life. This is why Krishna advises Arjuna to surrender his habitual pattern of becoming to the timeless cycle of being:

> Whatever you do, Arjuna, whatever you eat, whatever you offer in sacrifice, whatever you give, whatever you practice in austerity, do it as an offering to Me.
>
> *(9.27)*

The *law of giving* can make Arjuna a Self-organizing open system. The call is for complete devotion to whatever one does in the course of a daily life. The advice is to educate one's actions to become acts of service to others. The dedication of whatever one eats, whatever one thinks, or whatever one does to an open-ended and unmanifest being will give us the supreme energy of success. Ultimately, what Arjuna must do is give up is his own idea and illusion of being a separate entity apart from his open-ended universe. This is the final offering and the last frontier of giving. Jesus also talked about the law of giving 2,000 years ago:

> Very truly I tell you, unless a grain of wheat falls into the earth and dies, it remains just a single grain; but if it dies, it bears much fruit.
>
> *(John 12:24)*

# LEADERSHIP IS AN ADVENTURE OF CONSCIOUSNESS

Arjuna wants to know how a leader can keep in touch with the timeless Self even as he deals with challenges that occur in specific time and space. Krishna answers that a true leader is in constant remembrance of the conscious awareness within himself in the midst of all the activities of the mind and body. Krishna embodies this conscious awareness that is the basis of the unity of life. Krishna describes himself as the innermost secret among all secrets, which is silence. He concludes his Self introduction by saying that whatever is glorious, powerful, or prosperous in this world has sprung from this conscious-Self principle.

## LEADING CONSCIOUSLY

The follower asked the timeless leader, who was known to be enlightened, "What do you do all day?"

The leader responded, "I wake up, have breakfast, reach the office, do my work, come back home, take a shower, and go to sleep at night."

The follower was surprised by what the leader had just said. He exclaimed, "That is exactly what I do every day."

The timeless leader said, "But there is a difference. When I wake up, I really wake up. When I sleep, I sleep. When I do my work, I do only my work. When I take a shower, I just take a shower."

"I don't get it. What is the real difference between you and me, then?" queried the follower.

The leader replied: "The difference is that when you wake up today, you are still lost in the thoughts of yesterday; when you sleep, you are lost in your dreams. When you do your work, your mind is not on your work but on the fruits of work. When you take a shower you are thinking of a holiday in the Bahamas."

A timeless leader brings the whole consciousness of who he is to what he does. His mind does not fragment his unbroken consciousness while he is engaged in some task. He is not led astray by his thoughts. The source of his power is his conscious presence in the here-and-now. He has realized that just as a seed has all the ingredients of a giant tree, a conscious moment has the entire potential of the future ingrained in it. Inside a solitary seed is hiding the trunk, the branches, the flowers, and the fruits of the tree. Even if we dissect a seed with the most precise instruments, we cannot see the future tree. Similarly, within the seed of a conscious moment lies the untraceable energy and intelligence of the timeless. This energy or intelligence cannot be grasped by even the finest instruments of the human constitution: it is perceived neither by the senses nor by the brain.

How does a leader establish himself in that conscious presence? Krishna says to Arjuna:

> I give the knowledge of this conscious presence to those who seek me with love.

*(10.10)*

The flame of conscious presence is lit up by the fuel of complete devotion to whatever one is doing at the moment. The leader says, "When I work, I work. When I take a shower, I take a shower." A timeless leader does not deflect his energy by making the present moment a steppingstone to an imagined future. He lives completely in the moment. His thoughts, feelings, and actions are synchronized to the one point of attention. This kind of living in the moment has the power and the potency of a seed that contains the mystery of a whole forest.

Krishna refers to the timeless moment as he concludes this sutra:

> I, the unchanging and the timeless, sustain and permeate the entire cosmos with just one fragment of my being.
>
> *(10.42)*

Krishna consciousness permeates the solidity of the mountain and the fluidity of the river. This consciousness energises our breath and activates our neural network. This consciousness is the essential energy that drives all phenomena. He is asking Arjuna to be devoted, not to the physical person called Krishna, but to this conscious energy that Krishna embodies.

## SILENCE: THE LANGUAGE OF TIMELESS LEADERSHIP

> Among secrets I am Silence.
>
> *(10.38)*

What Krishna describes as the best-kept secret is the conscious principle called *silence*. Usually we associate secrecy with silence of speech. However, the timeless secret that Krishna is referring to is not only unspoken but also unspeakable—this secret is inaccessible to the senses. Silence is the secret source of all language. The state of silence is not merely emptiness of sound; it is the fullness of unspoken intelligence. Silence is the pure potentiality of language. Words and sounds are material expressions of this potentiality. Just as the choppy and noisy surface waves of the sea are held together by the vast, unruffled depths of water, silence integrates language into meaning and understanding. Silence can be harnessed when we learn to be observers rather than interpreters. When a leader observes without the urge to judge or interpret, he is bringing his whole attention to whatever he observes. This whole attention is silence.

Timeless leaders apply the discipline of silence by learning to be observers. Observation is the art of seeing without judging, naming, or measuring. One president of a multinational organization says that the only way he can get his organization to go to the next step of innovation is by enabling the organization to look at the business in entirely new ways. This requires breaking through the barriers of conditioned perception about the product, service, or the market. The CEO of a global hotel chain makes it a point to remain a silent observer in strategy meetings for as long as possible. He takes care not to even nod or shake his head, either to approve or disapprove a colleague's point of view. Thus, he resists the need to come to any conclusion prematurely. The practice of the art of silence helps leaders to seek knowledge from multiple sources. It enhances their range of options from which to make decisions.

Silence is nothing but this pure, unconditioned, and conscious intelligence that Krishna refers to as the *secret*. It is the basic foundation of a leader's understanding of reality. Silence is the ground of emergent language. To put it in terms of modern physical science, fluctuations of energy and information on the ground of silence create thoughts. Thoughts are nothing but molecules in motion—they are conditioned to flow in a certain pattern through the neural network. They are like the predetermined circuit in the neural network. Thoughts come from memory. If there were no memory there would be no thought. If we imagine the neural network in the brain to be the switchboard, then thoughts are the pre-planned circuit. However, neither the switchboard nor the circuit are of any use unless there is a flow of electricity through them. Silence is this flow of electricity.

Freedom of expression has two dimensions: freedom of speech and freedom of silence. Freedom of speech allows us to say what we feel is appropriate. Freedom of silence enables us to explore the deeper voices within us that speak to us without inhibition. Exercising the freedom of speech involves a much greater expenditure of energy compared to the freedom of silence. In speech, energy fragments into verbal expressions that are nothing but vibrations of sound energy. In silence, energy is integrated into noiseless awareness. If one holds back the urge to talk from time to time, one will experience a surge of energy in the nervous system. Silence is energy conserving. Therefore, a timeless leader consciously cultivates the discipline of silence.

The world of Nature is full of language. Nature communicates not through verbal expression but through unheard sounds and unseen vibrations. The flower announces its meeting schedule to the bee by means of the subtle vibration of its fragrance. The housefly declares a conference by buzzing its wings. The bat hears the vibrations of trees and conducts its business in the silence of the night. Silence is perpetually speaking to us. It is the most effective language known in Nature's organization, and enables it to execute its tasks without much resistance.

One of the most important issues in leadership development is the ability to make the right choices. A leader has to make many significant choices in the course of his life and work. A wise leader knows that choices are made in the space and time that exist between a certain stimulus and an appropriate response. For example, a business leader working for an insurance company is faced with a dilemma; she has to decide within five minutes whether she should insure a particular business. She has collected all the relevant data relating to this particular business and studied it carefully. Yet she is indecisive; she is unable to figure out whether it will be good business or bad business for her company. As she debates the pros and cons of the two possible choices before her, time is running out. At this point, she sits in silence with her eyes closed and ponders deeply. Then she makes the decision.

Many of us make decisions and choices in this way. We take stock of our thoughts about the possible consequences of the choices we might make. The greater the stakes involved in making the choice, the greater is the division of our thoughts into opposite camps. One group of thoughts marshals support for why a certain choice has to be made. Another group of thoughts gives us equally convincing reasons why a particular choice should not be made. An uncultivated mind is swayed by one group of thoughts or by the other, and then decides on the spur of the moment. But a mind that has learned the discipline of silence examines all the thoughts and after a while quietly slips into the silent gap between the thoughts. In this silence, the right choice is made with effortless ease.

## THE DYNAMISM OF INDIVISIBILITY

An organization is much more than the sum total of its material and intellectual assets. The whole is more than the sum of its parts. The whole is not a collection of parts but the indivisible relationship that exists among the parts. If we take all of the words in a sentence and change their order, the whole sentence will be destroyed. Even though the words remain the same, the order in which they are placed creates the meaning of the sentence. Meaning is not created by the words alone but by the indivisible relationship that exists between the words. If we compare an organization to a sentence, then the indivisible relationship among its various parts may be described as the ethos of the organization. The *ethos* is the collective script of the organization. It signifies the values that the organization stands for. Ethos gives meaning and wholeness to the organization. Even while dealing with various parts of the organization a timeless leader has his conscious attention attuned to the ethos.

The dynamic leader of the Tata Group, Mr. Ratan Tata, understands the importance of ethos as that indivisible principle that helps an organization grow. Mr. Tata inherited from his predecessors the ethos of the *trusteeship*—the organization that holds the trust of its stakeholders. The greatest wealth creator in India, Mr. Tata was paradoxically the man who gave to his country the cheapest car that the country's not-so-affluent people could afford. Ratan Tata reiterates his commitment to the indivisible ethos that binds his organization in the following principles:

1. Ensure that the company listens to the community around it and contributes to its well being.
2. Avoid all corrupt activities even when times are difficult and temptation is high.

In a country that is now committed to fighting widespread corruption, the Tata brand stands tall among its many competitors that have more readily succumbed to corrupt corporate practices. It is the core values of the Tata Group and its strong ethos that have been for a long time the central organizing principle. This principle has been responsible for the global impact of the brand, embracing a multitude of products and services.

As with its indivisible ethos, an organization builds its commercial identity on a set of core products or businesses. The Self-organizing corporation, however, goes beyond the products themselves in search of new relationships between its products and the people they serve. Sony had its commercial identity in the business of tape recorders and headphones. Yet, the power of Self organization within Sony built a new product based on the relationship between the tape recorder and headphones—the Walkman. The Walkman was the beginning of a new relationship between Sony and its customers. The Self-organizing capability of computer technology has built bridges of relationships between computers and communication, computers and transportation, computers and management, and so on.

Thus we can see that the indivisible Self or identity of a person, an organization, or even a technological product carries the dynamism that helps it grow in many dimensions. Krishna is alluding to this dynamism of indivisibility when he says to Arjuna:

> I am the source of all the spiritual and material worlds.
>> Everything emanates from my Self-organizing essence.
>> The wise who perfectly know this devote themselves to this essence.

> *(10.8)*

The whole of Nature is an example of the dynamism of indivisibility. On the surface, the mountain, the desert, and the ocean may appear to be separate from each other. Yet, they are inseparably connected to each other in the ecology of the universe. The same Earth that constitutes the height of the mountain also creates the depth of the seabed. The whole of our ecology is one seamless Self-organizing principle. It is this principle that makes Nature such a dynamic entity. Timeless leaders have an intuitive grasp of the ecology of the organization. They view the organization not as a totality of commercial assets but rather in the wholeness of its connection with the larger society, community, and environment that it chooses to inhabit. This indivisible relationship that the organization has with its larger ecology is what creates social capital for the organization.

A timeless leader understands that an organization's dynamism is reflected not only in the stock exchanges but also in the amplitude of its relationship with its whole ecology. It is this relationship that creates real wealth for the organization.

## THE PURSUIT OF EXCELLENCE

> Whatever is glorious, splendid, or powerful in any being, know that as a manifestation of a part of my brilliance.
>
> *(10.41)*

Krishna is stating something that runs contrary to our deeply held belief about human nature. Our lifelong education leads us to believe that we are inherently imperfect. As a result of this belief we seek imperfection instead of seeking excellence everywhere. Richard Branson, the well-known CEO and path-breaking British entrepreneur, echoes the pursuit of excellence as his business philosophy:

> You shouldn't be looking for people slipping up, you should be looking for all the good things people do and praising those.

Krishna does not offer the pursuit of excellence as a mere theory. Rather, he draws the attention of Arjuna to the many visible and tangible manifestations of His excellence in action:

> Among the immovable things I am the Himalayas.
>
> *(10.25)*
>
> Among men I am the King.
>
> *(10.27)*
>
> Among animals I am the Lion.
>
> *(10.30)*
>
> Among Sciences I am the Science of Self.
>
> *(10.32)*

I am the prosperity of those who become prosperous.

*(10.34)*

Among the seasons I am the flowery spring.

*(10.35)*

I am the victory in the victorious.

*(10.36)*

I am the industry in the determined.

*(10.36)*

I am the goodness of the good.

*(10.36)*

This is not a narcissistic claim. Krishna clearly says that a leader's journey of excellence begins with the awareness of excellence all around him. A timeless leader must examine with the eye of excellence everywhere he looks and everything he perceives. Excellence is first about *quality of mind* and awareness. Professional excellence is a result of developing quality of mind through constant awareness. This is different from expertise or efficiency. A lot of experts have almost blind allegiance to their expertise. Experts tend to think of themselves as those who have finally reached their goal. Those in pursuit of excellence are always beginners. Excellence is a journey without a finish-line. The journey of excellence begins every day with a new awakening and a newer insight that enriches the mind.

The pursuit of excellence is a timeless journey. Unlike the pursuit of a degree or a skill, there is no endpoint for excellence. The journey of excellence requires an unstinted commitment to lifelong learning. Even while he was the successful CEO of high-performing company Kimberley-Clark, Darwin Smith (1926–1995) was heard to say, "I never stopped trying to be qualified for the job." Under his leadership, Kimberley-Clark outperformed such venerable companies as Procter & Gamble, Coca-Cola, and General Electric, and grew more than four times compared to the average market performance.

The conscious Self-organizing and Self-learning principle to which Krishna is drawing Arjuna's attention is the basis of all forms and colours of excellence. Whether in the perfection of the shape of a flower or in the flowering of human intelligence, the Self-organizing principle evolves all species in Nature toward excellence. This conscious Self slowly reveals itself to a leader through lifelong learning. The timeless leader's job is to induce the spirit of accelerated learning in his protégé, Arjuna. Krishna helps broaden Arjuna's awareness to be appreciative of excellence everywhere and to emulate it. Whatever we appreciate eventually appreciates and grows within us. To learn to appreciate excellence is the starting point of the journey of excellence. Just as learning has no end but has only a beginning, the pursuit of excellence is a timeless and lifelong quest:

A world-renowned musician was bowing to accept a standing ovation for his extraordinary performance. After all the applause was over, a young woman shook the musician's hand and gushed, "I would give my life for such an excellent performance." The maestro smiled as he said, "I indeed gave my whole life for it!"

# SUTRA 11

# TIMELESS LEADERS HAVE INTEGRAL VISION

Arjuna wants to see the cosmic form of Krishna in one place, all at once. Krishna says it is impossible to see His cosmic form with the ordinary eyes of a mortal. Krishna therefore bestows upon Arjuna the divine vision that enables Arjuna to see the most extraordinarily horrific and terrific aspects of cosmic life. He sees, in a flash of insight encompassing the timeless, the spectacle of the death and destruction of his near-and-dear ones. Arjuna goes through a range of emotions from terror, to wonder, to gratitude. Unable to bear the intensity of this experience, Arjuna pleads with Krishna to restore to him his normal sight. Finally, Krishna reassures Arjuna that through unswerving service and devotion without attachment to the ego, the divine grace can be obtained.

## INTEGRAL VISION

What would happen if the leader of an organization were given magical powers to see everything happening within his world at any point in time? Wouldn't that be too much data for his eyes and mind to process? Yet many leaders aspire to see though the mind's eye that which their physical eyes are unable to see. The art of seeing though the mind's eye is often described as *visionary leadership*. Here is one example:

Two managers of Disneyland are walking through a Disney theme park. It was Disney's dream to see that park built during his lifetime, yet the park was constructed after he had passed away. One of the managers said to the other, "I wish Disney had lived to see this park." The other replied, "Disney saw it while he was alive." This kind of seeing involves *foresight*—the gift of being able to see something before its time. Foresight gives us the power to creatively reconstruct our universe by connecting the dots that are visible in the present.

One of the virtues of timeless leadership is the ability to recognize patterns based on inadequate or insufficient data points. The minds of these leaders work like radar screens scanning the environment for data and constructing patterns of intelligible information. India's ascent from a grossly poor country to one of the economic powerhouses of the world occurred when some of its best entrepreneurs recognized that the old pattern of thinking in India about "removal of poverty" was slowly giving way to "creation of wealth." This new pattern of thinking generated a wave of entrepreneurial activity that has now scripted India's growth story. In China, too, the patterns of thinking shifted from communist idealism to socialist market economy wherein leaders recognized that it was much more meaningful to distribute wealth to the citizens than to distribute poverty. Chinese statesman Deng Xiaoping highlighted this shift toward pragmatism from stubborn ideology as he said, "No matter if it is a white cat or a black cat; as long as it can catch mice, it is a good cat." The rise of China has much to do with this comprehensive shift in the pattern of thinking.

Timeless leaders have an integral vision of the changing faces of reality. They are able to sense a turning of the tide and to transmit this sense to their followers. Krishna says to Arjuna:

> You are not able to behold Me with your own eyes.
> I give you this divine vision; now behold the whole.
>
> *(11.8)*

This "Me" that Krishna refers to is a vision of wholeness that comes in a flash of insight. Krishna tells Arjuna: "It may not be possible for you to view the whole reality unfolding through you and around you with your ordinary optical instrument. Therefore, let me give you another perspective, another kind of sight." This kind of sight is referred to as *darshan* or world-view. In *darshan* one sees life in its many dimensions. Krishna gives Arjuna 3D glasses as it were to experience the spectacle that he is about to witness.

What does Arjuna see in the body of Krishna with his divine vision?

> I see You of boundless form on every side, with many arms, stomachs, mouths, and eyes; neither the end nor the middle nor the beginning do I see; O, Lord of the Universe, O, Cosmic Form.
>
> *(11.16)*

Arjuna sees all this as he looks at the body of Krishna. This is like seeing the whole universe in a grain of sand and the macrocosm in the microcosm. Krishna induces in Arjuna not just bewilderment but reverence for life. It is this reverence for the indivisible life that gives us the big picture. It is like the CEO of a company who is able to sense everything happening within his organization and outside it. When timeless leaders see the big picture, their thoughts and actions become synchronized in a manner that serves the larger purpose of their work.

What else does Arjuna see as he looks at the big picture? He sees that the warriors arrayed on the battlefield are getting annihilated in a horrific spectacle of death and destruction. The evanescence of the many forms of life and the inevitability of the death of the body render Arjuna terror stricken.

Arjuna sees the timeless dance of life: the emergence and birth of bodies and their merging back into the jaws of death. The mightiest of the heroes on the opposing side who Arjuna was dreading to fight are now killed by the passage of time. Krishna releases Arjuna from attachment to his own body as he confronts death—his enemies' as well as his own. All of our fears of life originate in just one fear: the fear of our own mortality. Once Arjuna is released from the fear of death, his fear of confronting his opposition in the battle also disappears. This is the essence of the integral vision that Krishna gives to Arjuna: the ability to see life and death as two sides of the same coin. Arjuna is now ready to fight without the fear of mortality. Krishna helps him see that a fighter becomes a true warrior when he learns to fight without the fear or hatred born of attachment to the body.

## SIGHT AND INSIGHT

The fighter fights with his sight; the warrior fights with *insight*. Aikido, a Japanese martial art, developed by Morihei Ueshiba, is an example of the use of insight. Aikido works on the principle that the energy of the opposition can be harnessed and integrated if the warrior has an integral vision of the fight. It is a path of unifying life's energy so that the warrior is willing and able to receive most of an opponent's attack even while staring death in the face. The warrior in Aikido sees an opponent's attack not in terms of linear physical movement but as circular energy. All that the warrior does is to move away from the line of attack so that he can use the opponent's energy to his advantage. An Akido master sums up the warrior's wisdom in the following way: "Sometimes the absence of the body is more important than the presence of mind."

Aikido training is mental as well as physical, emphasizing the ability to relax the mind and body even under the stress of dangerous situations. Krishna is like an advanced Aikido master asking Arjuna to look at his opposition not just as physical forms but as a movement of circulating energy in which forms appear and disappear to support and sustain that energy cycle. Arjuna acknowledges this as he sees his opposition merging into the larger amplitude of life, just as many rivers merge into the ocean:

> Truly, as many torrents of rivers flow toward the ocean,
>> So these heroes of our world enter Your flaming mouths.
>>>> *(11.28)*

Krishna's gift to Arjuna is the gift of insight, like an instant flash of lightning that opens the eyes of perception to a new reality. Insight comes not from memory but from unconditioned awareness. Insight shows us new faces of reality in a way that alters our maps of the universe forever:

> A tourist had gone to see Niagara Falls in Canada. He went there because he had heard a lot about Niagara from fellow travelers from around the world. He had heard legendary tales about this masterpiece of Nature. It was in the middle of winter when this tourist drove all by himself to see Niagara Falls. Unfortunately, he could see nothing particularly memorable there. Disappointed, he decided to drive back home. On his way back he dropped by an artist's studio. There he saw a huge painting of Niagara Falls in full flow. The picture so arrested his attention that he was

compelled to drive back to see Niagara again. Sure enough, this time he saw something magical now that the artist had opened his mind's eye!

Insight comes not from programmed thoughts but from the underlying source of all thought, which is consciousness. Imagine thoughts as tube-wells that draw water from the subsoil of the Earth. The underground water is like the stream of consciousness. If the flow of water in these tube-wells is clogged or choked for any reason, we will not receive any water. Likewise, when the perennial flow of consciousness is constricted by conditioned thinking and habitual modes of perception and action, we will be devoid of insight. Without insight a leader's sight becomes passive, like visual rag-picking. While sight dissects the world into parts, insight *integrates the parts* into a whole. Krishna opens up Arjuna's fragmented consciousness to the unity and interdependence of all life even as he faces the horror of death in battle.

## THE PANGS OF PLURALITY

There in the body of Krishna, Arjuna saw the whole Universe resting in One with all its infinite parts.

*(11.13)*

The view of the fighter is partial. He sees only his own part of the battle. Driven by his ego, he is obsessed with defending his own position against the enemy's attack. The fighter has little understanding of the whole battle. The ego's obsession is about the survival of the body and its continuity as a form. The fighter fights for his body and with his body. Just as he sees himself as separate from his opponent in body, he sees himself as separate in mind. Out of this sense of separation in the body and the mind, the emotions of aggression, dominance, and fearfulness arise. This is how the fighter prepares himself for violence, which is the inevitable result of this separation.

In contrast, the consummate warrior sees the same battle-field from another plane of awareness. The warrior is not obsessively attached to his part in the battle. He therefore plays his part with minimum attachment. The warrior is like both the scriptwriter and actor in his own play. The script-writer knows how the drama will resolve itself—therefore, he is not worried about how everything will turn out.

To use another analogy, the circus clown who entertains children by wearing different masks and impersonating animals is not frightening to children. The kids know that the man hiding behind the fearful mask is merely a human being like themselves. The kids enjoy a different range of emotions looking at the masks, but they are never caught in the illusion that the masks represent. The mask is apparent while the human face behind it is real. When leaders are able to dis-criminate between the real and the apparent they are free of emotional turmoil.

When leaders get caught in the illusion of their own sep-arateness in the battle of life they suffer the pangs of plurality. They cannot fight without vengeance, fear, and attachment to their turf. When leaders perceive only plurality without the underlying unity in plurality they become unnecessarily com-bative. The real test of an evolving leader is his ability to func-tion in a fiercely competitive field and yet nurture the cooperative and compassionate nature within himself. Such leaders are able to hold these two paradoxically opposite stances while going into a combat-like situation. Krishna tries to inculcate in Arjuna what American novelist F. Scott Fitzgerald described as first-rate intelligence: the ability to hold two opposite ideas in the mind at the same time, and still retain the ability to function.

How does the fighter Arjuna reconcile the illusion of having a separate body with continuing to see the oneness of spirit that connects him with his adversaries? How does he reconcile the fighter's mental preparedness to wreak havoc on the enemy with the warrior's equanimity and compassion for the other? Krishna teaches Arjuna how to stand apart from his ego and apart from his body-mind complex so that Arjuna is able to see himself as that cosmic consciousness that is whole, integral, and spiritual.

The incredible vision of Krishna as the cosmic creator, preserver, and annihilator without a beginning or an end gives Arjuna the perspective of the whole stream of life. When Arjuna's ego is caught in this vast and flowing whirlpool, he experiences anxiety, fear, and attachment to the life of his body and mind. Krishna further tells Arjuna that this form, this face, and this life are nothing more than an appearance in the stream of cosmic life. The goal of a fighter is to get out of this whirlpool of emotions that attachment brings and view life from the larger standpoint. If the fighter wants to be a warrior, then he has learn to see his separate existence as no more than an expression of the whole. Even while he is engaged in conflict in the physical world, the warrior has to do away with the conflict and restlessness in the psychological world. This is the paradox that the warrior has to negotiate. He can do that only when he learns to see himself as an instrument of the whole.

## THE LEADER AS SERVANT: BEING AN INSTRUMENT OF THE WHOLE

Gandhi wrote in his autobiography, "The best way to find your Self is to lose yourself in the service of others." A timeless leader can discover his sovereign and essential Self when he is able to let go of his preoccupations with his own body and mind. He can then be an instrument of the whole. This is exactly what Krishna urges Arjuna to do:

> Therefore, stand up and conquer your enemies, Arjuna.
>
> I am the mighty world destroying Time, now engaged in destroying the worlds.
>
> Even without you, Arjuna, none of the warriors arrayed in hostile armies shall live.
>
> Be merely an instrument of the whole.
>
> *(11.33)*

The enemies that Krishna is asking Arjuna to conquer are the army of thoughts and emotions commanded by his ego. Krishna is trying to dispel any notion that Arjuna may have about his own role in having to vanquish a formidable opposition that stands before him in the form of Kauravas. Krishna clearly conveys to Arjuna that Kauravas will lose the war and Arjuna's enemies will be destroyed by the sheer forces of cause and effect: They will reap what they have sown by way of their evil deeds. Thus, Arjuna need not have doubts about the outcome of the war; nor does he need to feel that he must himself ensure that outcome. The outcome of a war of this magnitude cannot be conceived or performed by an individual's thoughts or actions. The outcome will be determined by the dynamism of a world that the limited mind cannot conceive.

Hence the call to be merely an *instrument* of the whole: A perfect instrument makes no claims to glory and takes no credit for the best of accomplishments. The most sophisticated telescope reveals the secret of the stars without drawing any attention to itself.

- The best of services come from faceless instruments.
- The most accomplished servant does his work unseen.

Timeless leadership comes not from control of material resources but from serving the very human source that creates those resources. Leaders who demand authority in return for favours done or who rent out their power to subordinates in exchange for subservience cannot lead for long. This kind of control-based leadership breeds dependence on whatever is controlled. Instead, when leaders choose to serve unconditionally they touch a deep chord in the consciousness of those whom they choose to serve. This process creates willing followers.

Servant-leaders do not start with the intent of charming or influencing people. Instead, they start with the intent of being as perfect an instrument of the whole as possible. In the process they become an integral part of the very source of what it means to be human. This is the basis of their influence.

# SUTRA 12

# LOVE IS THE LEADER'S ESSENCE; LOVE IS THE LEADER'S PRESENCE

Arjuna asks Krishna about the path and practice of devotion. He wonders which of the two is better: to be devoted to the form of the divine or to his formless essence? Krishna explains that a devotee draws his inspiration from the source of love that integrates the human and the divine. A devotee's work therefore becomes love made visible. Krishna is telling Arjuna, "Do not try to manipulate the result of your work in the direction of what you alone would like the work to be. Do not dedicate your attention to the urges of your ego. When you renounce your need for censure or praise from the outside world, you will acquire a silence and steadiness of devotion to your work. That's when you will come close to me. That's when you would be dear to me."

135

## LEADERSHIP IS LOVE MADE VISIBLE

Bill George, former CEO of Medtronic, now a Harvard professor who teaches a popular course called Authentic Leadership, says to his class, "You have a choice between seeking the world's esteem and being grounded in your own intrinsic desire." One can hear in Bill's assertion the echoes of what Krishna advises Arjuna on the art of becoming an ideal devotee:

> A true devotee works independently of the world outside and draws his inspiration, equanimity, and ecstasy from the source within himself.
>
> *(12.16)*

Bill George is not unlike many other CEOs who discover that the journey from the head to the heart is one of the most difficult and most profoundly evolutionary leaps that a leader can make. Almost 15 years ago, I heard Bill in his role as CEO speaking to some mid-career executives. He was quoting to them this passage of Kahlil Gibran as though he were saying an earnest prayer:

> Work is love made visible. And if you cannot work with love but only with distaste, it is better that you should leave your work and sit on the gate of the temple and take alms of those who work only with joy.
>
> *(Gibran Kahlil,* The Prophet, *Alfred A. Knopf, New York, 1970)*

Krishna is guiding Arjuna through the path of devotion or *bhakti*. Devotion is nothing but love in action. Timeless leaders become aware of love in action as they become rooted in their intrinsic quest for love as a state of being. Timeless leaders know that if work is creation, then love is the creative impulse behind it. Such leaders trace the mysterious source of love not in the world of approval and disapproval but within their own hearts. Love in this case is not a mere feeling present on the surface of experience. Krishna traces the path of devotion and love to the depth of being and to the ultimate source of all meaningful actions.

Take the example of an organizational leader who wants his employees to focus on customer service. He goes at it hammer-and-tongs to make customer service the top priority while neglecting the fact that his own employees have to work odd hours in very poor working conditions. The employees may still provide reasonable customer service, but such service is unlikely to be inspiring. If you were a customer of such an organization, think about which you would prefer:

- The employees who provide the service truly love their work, and good customer service is the natural consequence of this devotion.
- The management of this organization has made it mandatory that employees must smile at customers even when the employees are unhappy with their working conditions.

It is likely that customers would prefer to receive the service from employees who provide it voluntarily, out of love of their work, rather than from employees who perform it under the not-so-subtle coercion of management.

Timeless leaders realize that while work is external to our state of being, love is an intrinsic state of our deeper human nature. Love is a state of consciousness and devotion in its psychological and physical expression. One can be truly devoted to work on a sustainable basis only when one can do so from the state of love. Krishna is teaching Arjuna the art and science of devoted work. It is easy for anyone to initiate desire for some work or other. However, to sustain the desire for such work requires devotion.

When a leader sets a very high goal for work it is necessary for him to maintain a state of high resolve and an unswerving devotion to the task at hand. This kind of devotion can come only if there is a perennial supply of energy from within the human constitution. It would be physically impossible to accomplish such great feats of human endeavour as building the Great Wall of China, conquering Mount Everest, or growing a successful multinational company unless there were sustained effort of an extraordinary kind. There is something intangible within the human constitution that makes it possible to sustain such high-energy work. The greatness of the effort actually comes from the intensity of love, which is the spirit behind the action. Timeless leadership is the manifestation of the invisible energy of love expressed through the visible medium of action.

All enduring and timeless work is nothing but love made visible. Love in the context of work is not a noun but a verb. Love is not merely about recognizing the objective value of a given task. Rather, it is the process of creating value from the inside out in any work we do. While in love, leaders seek what they value and value what they seek. Paying attention to detail, giving greater energy to the process rather than the output, and being fully present in the work are the foundations of love in action. When leaders do small work with great love their work automatically becomes great. Bill George describes this as follows: "The light shines in you, and you let others see it as well."

## DEVOTION: THE ART AND PRACTICE OF LEADERSHIP

Arjuna's question to Krishna is whether it is more profitable to be devoted to a concrete and manifest form of Krishna or to the formless transcendental essence of his divinity. Krishna responds by saying:

> Fix your mind on me only. Place your intellect in me. Then, you shall live in me alone.
>
> *(12.8)*

Krishna perceives that it is very difficult for Arjuna to be devoted to the formless aspect of divinity while Arjuna's mind is still caught up in the physical world of the senses. Krishna recognizes that Arjuna is where his mind is. If the mind is caught in the whirlpool of wishing and willing, of desires and doubts, it cannot devote itself to the highest, formless truth. Whereas appraising the formless requires extraordinary discrimination and detachment, Krishna prescribes to Arjuna the simpler path of devotion and dedication of all his mental energies to his mentor. Complete devotion to a form, as Krishna suggests, eventually leads to the awareness of the formless. The following story illustrates the point:

> A leader had gone to his spiritual mentor, seeking advice on how to improve his relationship with a particularly difficult co-worker. His mentor told him: "For the first fifteen days, simply listen to every word that your co-worker speaks. Be careful not to miss a single word!"
>
> The leader followed his mentor's instruction and came back after a couple of weeks, reporting a slight improvement in the relationship.
>
> "Now, said the mentor, for the next fifteen days, listen to everything that your co-worker has left unsaid between the words."
>
> Two weeks later, the leader reported that this had created a deep understanding between him and his co-worker.

Just as words and silence integrate to create understanding, both the form and the formless create the fabric of truth.

Krishna is inviting Arjuna to fix his mind on the truth that Krishna embodies. Ordinarily, our minds are fixed on our likes and dislikes. Whatever we like engages us and what we dislike repels us. Most leaders spend time doing what they like to do rather than what should be done. Krishna says that Arjuna should control the mind to keep it from fluctuating between likes and dislikes by meditating on the form of Krishna. The meditator can control the mind only by standing apart from the mind and by identifying himself with that power of the sovereign Self that can rule over and direct his mental energies. The mind is monitored by the discriminating intellect and the intellect is empowered by the sovereign Self. This sovereign Self is like the "uninterrupted power supply" (UPS); the intellect is the software and the mind is the hardware. The software directs the hardware only when the UPS is activated.

Just as someone flying in an airplane places complete trust in the pilot and sleeps peacefully during the flight, Krishna says, "Arjuna, entrust the reins of your mind and intellect to me." In essence, Arjuna is advised to hold the likes and dislikes of his personal self in abeyance out of devotion and love to the impersonal and sovereign Self that Krishna embodies. The sovereign Self is the pilot that can steer Arjuna's mind and intellect in the right direction. When Arjuna is able to establish his trust in the Self, his mind will not be hijacked by the multiple distractions of the world of likes and dislikes. This state of mind is defined by Krishna as:

> He by whom the world is not agitated and who cannot be agitated by the world.
>
> He who is free from likes and dislikes, envy, fear, and anxiety.
>
> *(12.15)*

A mind that is free from the pangs of likes and dislikes will naturally be drawn to a state of equanimity. In the course of

meeting people and getting work done within the organization, a leader acquires many defence mechanisms within the
mind. Such a mind is a bundle of agitations. A defensive mind
is hell-bent on domination of other minds; it is indifferent
and insensitive to the world beyond its conception. A leader
with such a mind can demoralize a lot of people through a
callous gesture or a cruel look. This kind of mind is incapable
of diligent and devoted work. Krishna suggests to Arjuna a
three-step way out of this messy mind-state:

1. Surrender to the highest intelligence that controls
   your mind and intellect.
2. Dedicate all that you do to the intelligence that gov-
   erns the universe and keeps the mighty planets whirl-
   ing in their orbits.
3. Trust this mighty intelligence to guide your mind
   and intellect in the most effective and efficient way.

Devotion is the means and love is the end of dedicated
work. Whatever we completely devote ourselves to occupies
us. If we devote ourselves to ignorance, then we grow in our
ignorance; if we devote ourselves only to that which we like,
we perpetuate our desire for our likes; if we devote ourselves
to the higher intelligence of love beyond likes and dislikes, we
begin to embody that love.

The ultimate evolution of leadership is a return to the
principle of love that holds an organization and its people
together. When we define love merely as a feeling, we do not
recognize the infinite organizing capacity of love in our
everyday lives. Timeless leaders see love as the common value
present in both competitive and cooperative frames of reference. In competition, love becomes merely the means to
achieving an end, as when we love our work because it will
fetch us greater rewards than our colleagues. In cooperation,
love becomes an end in itself, as when we love doing work
for our families for no other reason than the sheer joy of

sharing our lives with others. When leaders grow in love they experience its evolutionary impulse in pushing them from a competitive to a cooperative mindset. Beyond cooperation, a leader experiences love purely as a law of being. The timeless leader Gandhi saw love as a law like gravity; he said that this law will work just as the law of gravitation works *whether we accept it or not.*

## ATTRIBUTES OF THE LEADER AS DEVOTEE

Krishna describes to Arjuna the attributes of a true devotee:

> One who goes beyond censure and praise, who is silent and steady-minded in his devotion—that man is dear to me.
>
> *(12.19)*

A leader who has one eye on praise and another eye on possible censure is certainly not attentive to the work at hand. Mr. Mukesh Ambani, one of India's best-known corporate leaders, says, "I base my decisions on what should be done, rather than what I would like to do." This is an example of devotion to the process of work rather than running after self-seeking behaviours based on pursuit of pleasure and avoidance of pain. Krishna tells Arjuna, "Do not try to manipulate the result of your work in the direction of what you alone would like the work to be. Do not dedicate your attention to the urges of your ego. Instead, work for the simple truth that your action is only a part of a larger and ampler process like a ripple in the ocean. When you renounce your need for censure or praise from the outside world, you will acquire a silence and steadiness of devotion to your work. That's when you will come close to me. That's when you would be dear to me." Krishna assures Arjuna when a leader rises above blame or praise for work, he evolves to his highest Nature and his deepest potential. In this state his work becomes worship.

The path of devotion is not about emotional excess. It is rather about dropping the emotional baggage of the mind toward a singularity of purpose. Devotion means discovering that creative source in our heart rather than acquiring the approval of the world. Devotion is about educating the body, mind, and senses to connect our deepest desire to that primal energy called *love*. Love is that wholeness that the leader can experience when he is able to subdue his senses, restrain the narrow acquisitiveness of the mind, and steady his intellect in the awareness of the divine presence within and around himself. In the presence of love alone the devotee is able to reclaim the divine inside the human.

The practice of devotion consists of these three steps:

1. The devotee sees himself as an instrument rather than as a *doer* of actions. He works with the attitude, "I work with the knowledge and the power of the sovereign Self that is the primary doer." He thus travels on the path without the extra baggage of ego and anxiety that comes from performance pressure.

2. When the devotee performs an action with a feeling of love and reverence for the sovereign Self, he brings greater energy to his action than if he were to do the same thing from a personal need or a sense of mechanical duty. Meaningful action is more energising than mechanical action.

3. The devotee practices giving up the obsession of gaining a particular result. When his heart is full, his wants reduce in number. The devotee then gains the knowledge that there are many different ways of getting to the result. "My way or the highway" may not always be the best way!

In the final analysis, the devotee seeks the freedom that comes from renunciation of the fruits of one's actions as guided by narrow self-interest. Such renunciation is like an individual wave dissolving into the ocean. In the psychological universe, what dissolves is merely the false notion that the devotee had of being an independent and separate actor. When this false notion dissolves into the ocean of wisdom, peace and evenness of mind surround the devotee like the calm depths of the deep sea.

Krishna takes Arjuna up the ladder of evolution by which a devotee moves from practice to wisdom. He says that superior to practice is the knowledge that the devotee acquires through practice. Superior to this knowledge is the insight that one gets by meditating on the real source of that knowledge. The insight is that a devotee is only a secondary knower and a secondary doer. The primary knower and doer is that sovereign Self. Finally, renunciation of the results of one's action to that Sovereign knower and doer brings wisdom and peace. This is the ultimate quest of all knowledge and action:

> Knowledge is indeed better than practice; meditation is better than knowledge; renunciation of the results of action is better than meditation; peace is the reward of those who follow renunciation.
>
> *(12.12)*

# SUTRA 13

# LEADERS COMMAND THEIR FIELD WITH THE EYE OF WISDOM

Arjuna pleads with Krishna to explain to him the distinction between the field of experience and the eternal knower of that field. Krishna describes the *field* as the entire network of material and mental forces that create our beliefs, guide our behaviour, and determine the business of our life—in short, all that can be known and observed constitutes the *field of all fields*. However, Krishna reminds Arjuna that the knower of this field is the eternal subject that observes the field without prejudice or psychological distortion. The ultimate fulfilment of a timeless leader is to be the *knower of his field*. A leader can be this knower when he integrates his head and heart and acquires those virtues that give him the *eye of wisdom*.

## THE LEADER AS A KNOWER IN THE FIELD OF KNOWLEDGE

Arjuna's request of Krishna is:

> The field of experience and the Knower of the field, knowl-
> edge and that which ought to be known, these, Krishna, I
> desire to learn.
>
> *(13.1)*

By the word *field*, Arjuna is referring to the context and content of his experience.

Leadership is a highly context-sensitive process. In order
to succeed, leaders have to understand their contexts. Krishna
begins to broaden Arjuna's understanding of the "field" or the
context of leadership:

> Listen to me on what that field is, what its properties are,
> and what are its many modifications.
>
> *(13.3)*

Before we listen to Krishna's exposition on the field, we
will ponder how a leader is linked with the field of business.
Ram Charan, world-renowned business author and one of
the most trusted advisors to CEOs, tells us: "It is not a great
CEO but it is actually a great fit between a CEO and a company's contextual needs that builds great organizations." To
illustrate this point, he quotes numerous examples of failed
CEOs that prove that a CEO's inability to make sense of the
context of work leads to his own and his organization's
downfall. For instance, large multinational organizations that
had appointed three consecutive CEOs with similar sales
backgrounds had failed to grow their businesses. This was
because these leaders' conditioned behaviour from their past

experience was inconsistent with the changing contexts of their business.

Leadership is an integral feature of an organization's social system. Leaders are influenced by and in turn exert an influence on the social and organizational contexts that they command. The reason why a successful leader in one organization or culture becomes a failure in another organization or culture is simply this: A leader not only grows within a culture but also carries a culture within himself.

In his answer to Arjuna's request, Krishna describes the field of timeless leadership as the entire phenomenal world. He describes this as "the field in all fields".

> Know me, Arjuna, as the Knower of the field in all fields.
> The knowledge of the field and its knower do I regard as true knowledge.
>
> *(13.2)*

The field of all fields includes all that we can be aware of—all objects, and all modifications of the mind such as likes and dislikes, misery, fortitude, knowledge, and ignorance. The progressive discovery of the various dimensions of the field constitutes *true knowledge* as described by Krishna. Therefore, true knowledge is not just about the objective but about the subjective as well. A leader pursuing true knowledge has to learn to be an observer not only of "the world out there" but also of all that happens "in here," inside his own mind. A CEO of a major manufacturing firm says:

> I am constantly watchful of the psychological distortions resulting from *how* I view the facts on the table rather than just *what* I am viewing. If my sales figures tell me that I am a market leader, my mind hides the fact that the reason I am the market leader is that our lead competitor has stopped manufacturing the product and has abandoned

the market. When my awareness is able to observe this distorting mechanism of the mind, I know what the sales figures on my table really mean.

The field of experience for a business leader is therefore not just the objective field of facts but also the subjective field of thoughts, perceptions, and emotions. All these thoughts, perceptions, and feelings become objects in the light of our awareness. They become content in the mirror of our awareness. In the course of a day a business leader has to go through a dizzying array of situations and an unimaginable variety of contexts. Given the dynamic nature of his business settings, a leader needs the conceptual depth that will help him understand and deal with ambiguities and inconsistencies. Herb Kelleher, the maverick CEO of Southwest Airlines, states how he deals with rapid changes in his field:

> We tell our people that we value inconsistency. By that, I mean that we are going to carry 20 million passengers this year and that I can't foresee all of the situations that will arise at the stations across our systems. So what we tell our people is: "Hey, we can't anticipate all of these things, you handle them the best way possible. You make a judgment and use your discretion, we trust you will do the right thing. If we think you've done something erroneous, we'll let you know—without criticism, without backbiting."
>
> *(Herb Kelleher, quoted in Julie M. Fenster,* In the Words of Great Business Leaders, *John Wiley & Sons, New York, 2000, p. 325)*

Krishna is alluding to the knower as someone who is able to oversee the sum total of the interactions in his field, both objective as well as subjective, without having to be physically present. This can be possible only if the leader knows and trusts the intelligence of his people and backs them to make the right decisions depending on their specific contexts. He thus has to possess an overarching awareness that helps him see his people as extensions of his awareness:

> With his hands and feet everywhere, with eyes, heads, and faces on all sides, with ears on all sides, the knower dwells in the world, enveloping all.
>
> *(13.13)*

The knower, with pure and limitless awareness, is thus able to comprehend ambiguities and reconcile contradictions in the field. Just as electricity can perform two apparently opposing functions such as cooling a refrigerator and heating an electric oven and yet remain the same electricity, this awareness of a leader enlivens a variety of conflicting contexts in a field and yet remains pure and unconditioned. Krishna is referring to this knower, who commands the field by being part of the field and yet transcending it:

> The knower is without and within all beings. He is unmoving as also moving. He is too subtle to be known. He is far away and yet He is near.
>
> *(13.15)*

## THE DIMENSIONS OF THE FIELD AND THE KNOWER OF THE FIELD

Just as electricity is one entity but its applications are many, the knower is one, but the field of the known has many dimensions. The knower is one awareness that is reflected in different people, depending on their physical and mental abilities. The knower thus is reflected differently by different dimensions of the field in the same manner that sunlight appears blue when it is reflected by the ocean and green when it is reflected by a forest.

A leader who commands the field has to be engaged in as well as detached from his field. This paradoxical state of *detached engagement* is much like pure light that shows up as blue or green on different surfaces and yet remains detached as pure light. A timeless leader achieves this detached engagement through the power of *empathy*. Empathy is not a mushy emotional state where the leader gets lost in pleasing everybody. Rather, empathy is a detached and objective appraisal of how another person is feeling. Through empathy, a leader is able to rise above his own emotional isolation and connect with a follower. A company is losing market share due to a gloomy downturn. There is one very pessimistic vice president in the firm who casts a deep gloom over all the managers by his negative emotional state. He announces imminent job cuts. Another vice president, in a different company also experiencing downturn, rises above his own despondency and promises to work shoulder-to-shoulder with his managers in making the best out of the worst times. He cheers up his troops by saying that he would share all critical information relating to company decisions with his people and see that no one is unjustifiably fired. This second vice president, needless to say, will command his field much more effectively.

Krishna tells Arjuna that the knower of the field is like a spectator watching a film. The spectator identifies with the actors and actresses playing their parts on the screen. He laughs and cries with the protagonists in the movie. Yet, he understands in the light of his intelligence that what looks like actors in the movie is nothing but the interplay of light and shadow on a white screen. Therefore, when the movie is over, the spectator gradually returns to his neutral self. His engagement with the film is followed by a state of detachment after he leaves the movie theater.

If the knower of the field is unconditioned awareness that engages and detaches spontaneously with the field, then Arjuna's question is: "What are the properties of the field that the leader is supposed to know about?" Krishna gives a comprehensive definition of the *field* to Arjuna. Krishna describes the field as the entire universe of (1) material and (2) mental objects that a leader can be aware of. Everything other than this unconditioned awareness becomes the *object* of the field. The constituents of the field include the physical body as well as the senses and sense objects—the mind with its various modifications such as desire, hatred, ego, pleasure, and pain. Krishna defines *unconditioned awareness* as the timeless and subjective knower—everything else that this subject can know is the field of knowledge.

The timeless leader as the knower is perennially alive and alert to whatever physical modifications and psychological distortions happen in his universe. Such a leader remains humble and rarely seeks the spotlight. He is the unseen seer and the unheard hearer of the condition of his people and the universe they populate. He is neither deceived by flattery from his inner circle nor aloof to the plight of those who are far away from him. Krishna tells Arjuna that all of this is possible once the leader begins to see with the eye of wisdom.

## SEEING WITH THE EYE OF WISDOM

Timeless leaders have the ability to see the invisible. Behind the visible universe of objects and events there is the invisible universe of beliefs, perceptions, and emotions. The more a leader becomes sensitive to these invisible elements in his field, the more he attains what Krishna describes as the eye of wisdom:

> Those who perceive thus by the eye of wisdom the distinction between the field and the knower of the field, they attain to the supreme intelligence.
>
> *(13.34)*

Discovery of the eye of wisdom, according to Krishna, is the ultimate fulfilment of a timeless leader's life. The eye of wisdom is nothing but the capacity of subtle discrimination that helps the leader discern the whole relationship between the field and the knower of the field. The eye of wisdom teaches a leader the craft of this supreme vision. Thomas Watson Sr., the founder of IBM, once said that no leader can escape supervision. In fact the president and general manager of every department are supervised more closely than the frontline salespeople. A leader understands that every member of his organization, including himself, is subject to scrutiny and observation by every other member. This awareness brings about deeper sensitivity in the leader as he begins to see the finer nuances in his field. He starts being aware of how his own attention moves not just to people and things but to the hitherto-unseen spaces between and behind people and objects.

Through this awareness a timeless leader sees how the human mind creates patterns of meaning out of the flux of life and how these mental patterns become behaviours and material objects. In short, the mental beliefs of a leader can affect an organization's behaviour and this collective behaviour affects business. Thus, the dynamic interplay of beliefs, behaviours, and business is what the leader sees as the field. Eventually, the leader's field becomes the projection of the mind. The leader sees only what he is used to seeing or what he expects to see from his memory. The neurons in his brain fire through the path of least resistance. The leader's vision is now stuck in the inert, material, and mental surface of reality. In order to reclaim the eye of wisdom, the leader must deepen his vision beyond the usual pattern of reaction in his cerebral structure. He must now start seeing with the eye of the heart.

The eye of wisdom can be discovered by the leader only when he can fully integrate his head and his heart. The journey from the head to the heart can be the most arduous discipline that a leader can undertake. This requires cultivation of those qualities that constitute the ethical core of timeless leadership. Krishna enumerates to Arjuna 12 qualities of a leader who has truly integrated the head and the heart:

1. Humility
2. Non-injury
3. Unpretentiousness
4. Forgiveness
5. Uprightness
6. Service to one's teacher
7. Purity
8. Steadfastness
9. Self-regulation
10. Absence of egoism
11. Even-mindedness
12. Seeking periodic solitude and silence

These qualities give the leader those subtle eyes that reflect reality without mental distortions and biases. Without these qualities a leader merely identifies himself with his functions, such as sensations, thinking, and feeling. He mistakes his mental reactions, ego, and fear as his reality. But when the eye of wisdom is discovered he reflects reality without the mask of appearances that are caused by excessive identification with his body and mind. The eye of wisdom reveals to him a mirror-like dweller inside his body-mind complex. This dweller is the timeless witness that observes everything without reacting. This witness does not distort pure perception with immediate judgement and emotional reaction. A timeless leader's first job is to witness what is real. His ultimate job is to act on that reality. Only when he sees and acts on what is real can a leader truly command his field.

# SUTRA 14

# LEADERS HARNESS THE DYNAMIC FORCES OF NATURE

Krishna teaches Arjuna the means of attaining perfection by harnessing the three forces of Nature—inertia, dynamism, and illumination—that run our physical and mental universe. Krishna describes how the human mind is an exquisite synthesis of these three psycho-physical forces. It is a leader's essential work to study these three forces as they play out in the mind and to balance them optimally so that the leader can function harmoniously in his world. However, Krishna unveils to Arjuna that real liberation of the embodied soul that is held hostage by these three forces can come about only when the leader transcends the mind and its fluctuating moods. This can come about through unswerving devotion to and love for the perfection inherent in our being.

# NATURE'S MANUSCRIPT:
# THE THREE FORCES

Krishna says, "Arjuna, I shall now reveal to you the ultimate knowledge, gaining which, all the sages have reached the ultimate destination of freedom from all bondage. All the sages knew the secret forces of Nature that bind the soul Self." He then proceeds to reveal the secret of Nature to Arjuna:

> Inertia, dynamism, and illumination—these three qualities of Nature bind and embody the indestructible soul in us.
>
> *(14.5)*

Nature's work is an exquisite synthesis of *inertia*, *dynamism*, and *illumination*. These are the three fundamental modes of expression in Nature. These three processes can be seen at work in both the physical and the psychological universe. Inertia is the state of passivity; it is the seed form of physical or psychological action. In inertia, life is turned inwardly before it can evolve outwardly. Dynamism, the second process, is the movement from non-action to action and from passivity to passion. It is the stage of the growth and evolution of form and phenomenon. Illumination, the third process, represents another dimension of evolution—the evolution of consciousness. Illumination is not so much growth in the physical realm as it is growth in the psychological realm.

The mineral world represents inertia. Rocks remain the same for millions of years; the change in them is too slow to be detected with our physical senses. The plant kingdom represents a gradual movement from inertia to dynamism. Plants are capable of rapid growth, but they still are rooted in one place. Their dynamism is static. Animal life, on the other hand, is more dynamic. Animals can change locations and thus manipulate their universe.

Illumination, the third quality of Nature, is something that is largely dormant in plants and is present in only a very rudimentary stage in the animal kingdom. In human beings we see the first real evidence of self-awareness. The power of conscious thought and action in the human universe comes from this illumination or self-awareness. To be completely self-aware is the highest expression of human evolution.

Nature is not a fixed position but a *disposition*. It is forever trying to evolve in a certain direction. Human nature is an accumulation of several dispositions or qualities. Inertia, which is a quality of the most primitive forms of life on earth, is manifested in human nature as laziness, indolence, and stagnation. It is antithetical to movement. Inertia is not necessarily dysfunctional, however, because it helps to conserve energy. A piece of land left fallow for a long time regains its fertility through inertia.

Dynamism, which is a visible feature of Nature's personality, lends impetus to action. Dynamism is the active principle behind regeneration in Nature. In the physical sense, it is the opposite of inertia. Whereas inertia is the force of preservation, dynamism is the agent of change. Human nature, which is dominated by dynamism, gives birth to action-persons. Cultures and countries that have a preponderance of dynamic men and women demonstrate great affluence—glittering cities, large industries, and technology-driven modes of living. Despite all its advantages, however, dynamism can be dysfunctional if it is not accompanied by illumination or the light of awareness. Dynamism without awareness is short-lived and fated to self-destruction. Roman civilization, which flourished on the basis of dynamic hedonism, collapsed like a house of cards in the absence of illuminated leadership.

How does dynamism evolve into the quality of illumination? This is one of the most remarkable secrets of Nature. The ancient masters of India understood that Nature, including human nature, evolves along two paradoxical paths. One is the path of *pravritti*, in which Nature exteriorizes its energy and bursts out into a riot of forms and shapes and colours. In the psychological universe of human beings, *pravritti* carves out the path of desire and ambition.

The second path of Nature is the way of *nivritti*. It is the interiorized and inward-looking energy in Nature. On this path, Nature hibernates, arrests growth, and pulls inward the energy that would otherwise be frittered away in outward expression. In the psychological sense, *nivritti* represents the force of introspection and mindfulness. When the outgoing dynamism of Nature is arrested temporarily by *nivritti*, the same dynamic energy curves back into itself and evolves into a power of greater subtlety. This energy assumes the quality of illumination. Just as an iron bar heated to a high temperature concentrates its heat energy into light, the energy of dynamism when sufficiently concentrated assumes the quality of illumination.

Light of awareness, or illumination, which is the third basic component in the evolution of a human being, marks the difference between the subhuman and animal aspects of human beings and their higher nature. With the dawning of Self awareness, a human being aspires to the higher strata of Nature's evolution. Intuition begins to function, and the person begins to manifest a certain clarity of vision and empathy with all living forms on earth. Illumination bestows a purposive direction to dynamism and infuses inertia with a positive energy for stabilizing the order of Nature.

## HOW LEADERS HARNESS THE THREE FORCES OF NATURE

In Nature, the principle and the process of leadership work together. The process is the visible relation between various aspects of Nature, and the principle is the underlying law that keeps these processes in order. Inertia, dynamism, and illumination are principles as well as processes. They determine the direction in which life will evolve in Nature and how it will do so.

Human beings have assumed leadership among all other species in Nature's kingdom by obeying the evolutionary principle of illumination or Self awareness. This has given them an edge over the dynamism of animal life and the inertia of the plant kingdom. At the same time, the human species is an unfinished process of Nature. Human life is still in the process of evolution toward the greater designs of Nature. This evolution is a progressive expansion and unfolding of consciousness.

A conscious leader makes creative use of the principles as well as the processes of inertia, dynamism, and illumination. A conscious CEO allows some problems to remain undecided because he is conscious that a certain amount of inertia is more useful in solving a problem than premature and aggressive action. He says, "I tend to let things sort themselves out. Nine problems out of 10 go away if you don't address them. You have to deal with the tenth. I often don't address things until I have to."

Leaders discover that the secret of right action is to allow the action to unfold at the right time rather than to force it ahead of its time. A wise leader can hold dynamism in check to gain illumination. Lao Tzu described the essence of this in these wonderful lines:

> Whosoever practices non-action, occupies himself with not being occupied,
>     Finds taste in what does not taste: he sees the great in the small and the much in the little.
> *(Richard Wilhelm and H.G. Oswald, trans.,* Lao Tzu,
> *Penguin Books, New York, 1995)*

Thus we see that the three forces of Nature that Krishna talks about play out in both the physical as well as the psychological world. The secret to harnessing the forces of Nature is to observe how these forces work in the human mind. When a leader begins to observe the movement of his thoughts, he discovers that these thoughts trigger different moods in the mind space. Attachment to these moods is the cause of his bondage. If a leader is prone to inertia, then he will be led by the dull and obscuring force of his mind. His mental faculties will be slothful. He would neither understand nor want to understand the reason for problems in his organization. If the same leader is caught up in the whirlpool of dynamism, then he will be restless to act on his prejudices. He will project his own solutions onto the problems in his organization. Very often these solutions will backfire because they are based on his own likes and dislikes. Finally, if the leader is guided by his mind of illumination, then he will begin to see things more and more as they really are. His solutions to problems will be based on a correct appraisal of reality.

- A mind guided by the force of inertia obscures reality and veils it.
- A mind guided by the force of dynamism projects reality through the ego and distorts it.
- A mind guided by the force of illumination discriminates and perceives reality correctly.

Yet, all these forces of Nature working through the mind serve a purpose if they are harnessed fully. It is evident that without illumination a leader cannot know anything correctly. Without the force of dynamism a leader cannot perform actions. Without the force of inertia a leader will not know how to rest in order to engage with actions with greater vigour. When these forces of nature work in harmony in the mind of a leader—he becomes truly effective.

Krishna warns Arjuna that all the three forces of Nature working though the mind can block human capacity if they are excessively present. He says:

> The force of illumination is light giving and healing; it binds with the ego of knowledge.
>
> *(14.6)*

> The force of dynamism is of the nature of passion; it binds with the attachment to action.
>
> *(14.7)*
>
> The force of inertia is born of ignorance, of mortal man's delusion; it keeps him bound in sloth and slumber.
>
> *(14.8)*

When a leader observes his mind he is able to see the psychological forces of inertia, dynamism, and illumination drifting like clouds in his mental space. He sees inertia like dark clouds in the form of dullness, delusion, fear, lethargy and constant forgetfulness. He observes dynamism in the form of excessive ambition, restlessness, passion, anger, impatience, stress and indulgence. He observes illumination like a clear sky where knowledge, understanding, purity, patience and forbearance play out.

A leader sees that inertia binds through attachment to inaction and dulled thinking. Inertia is good when one is in a state of sleep. However, when he is awake and working, a leader has to harness an excess of inertia by converting it into the force of dynamism by physical exercise and mental exertion. Similarly, when dynamism becomes excessive it leads to hectic action and its consequent results and there is greed for more of the same. A leader can check this greed by the force of illumination that brings greater discrimination in one's action. A successful leader and president in an academic institution says,

> There are times I have to push back decision making to my subordinates when they are too slothful and do not take decisions that they are supposed to take on their own. Sometimes I have to go ahead and do it all by myself when I am required to lead from the front. On some other occasions I have to discriminate and figure out exactly when I must push back decision making and when I must act on my own.

These three states of mind represent the balancing of the forces of inertia, dynamism, and illumination.

# TRANSCENDING THE DYNAMICS OF NATURE

Krishna holds out to Arjuna the promise of fulfilment if he is able to rise above the three forces of Nature by striking the perfect equilibrium between the forces of inertia, dynamism and illumination. Just as an athlete gets into a zone of peak performance when he finds perfect rhythm in his running, a leader discovers a zone of his own when he transcends the dynamics of Nature and reaches a state of perfection.

> Crossing beyond the forces of Nature, which owe their being to the body, the embodied soul released from the bondage of birth, death, age, and pain attains freedom and immortality.
>
> *(14.20)*

The journey of a timeless leader through the wilderness of the three forces of Nature and his homecoming to the perfection of his soul is best illustrated by an Indian parable related by a nineteenth-century Indian sage, Shri Ramakrishna:

> Once, a leader was going through a forest, when three robbers waylaid him and robbed him of all his belongings. One of the robbers said, "What's the use of keeping this man alive?" So saying, he was about to kill him with his sword, when the second robber interrupted him, saying: "Oh, no! What is the use of killing him? Tie his hands and feet and leave him here." The robbers bound his hands and feet and went away.
>
> After a while the third robber returned and said to the man: "You see, I feel a little guilty. I hope we haven't hurt you much? I will release you from your bonds." After setting the man free, the third robber said: "Come with me. I will take you to the public highway."
>
> After a long journey through the forest they reached the road. At this the man expressed his gratitude: "Sir, you have been very good to me. Come with me to my house."

"Oh, no!" the robber replied. "I can't go there. My journey ends here."

This world of matter and mind itself is the forest. The three robbers prowling here are illumination, dynamism, and inertia. It is they who rob a man of the Knowledge of Truth. Inertia wants to destroy him. Dynamism binds him to the world. But illumination rescues him from the clutches of inertia and dynamism. Under the protection of the wisdom of illumination, man is rescued from anger, passion, and the other evil effects of the other two forces. Further, illumination loosens the bonds of the world. But illumination too is a robber. It cannot give man the ultimate Knowledge of Truth, though it shows him the road leading to the perfection of being, which is a human being's final destination. Setting him on the path, illumination tells him: "Look beyond the forest. There is your home."

*(Ramakrishna,* The Gospel of Shri Ramakrishna, *Ramakrishna Ashram, Kolkata, 1998)*

The leader in the parable is the soul Self of a leader who is waylaid by three forces of Nature: inertia, dynamism, and illumination. Of these three forces, the power of illumination gives him the closest view of his identity—his soul Self that is his original home. Yet even as the leader yearns to take home with him the desire for illumination and wisdom, that desire, too, binds him. This binding is like staying in a golden cage—however precious, it is still a cage. The desire for knowledge and wisdom, too, holds the leader a hostage to the material plane.

Arjuna's urge to transcend the binding forces of his own nature is aroused by Krishna. Arjuna therefore asks:

What are the characteristics of those who have gone beyond the barriers of Nature, O Krishna? How do they act? How have they passed beyond the clutches of Natural forces?

*(14.21)*

Krishna replies that truly liberated souls are unmoved by the harmony of illumination, the activity of dynamism, or the delusion of inertia. He further says:

> Those who transcend their own nature are not disturbed by the actions of the forces of nature. They know that it is these forces of nature that act and that the soul Self within is a mere witness to these actions. They therefore remain unshaken and abide within themselves.
>
> *(14.23)*

When a leader is caught in the bind of Nature he is obsessively stuck in his own body and identified with the fleeting moods of his mind. This diminishes the leader's influence. But when the leader goes beyond his body-mind obsession he transcends the limitations of his personality. He is no longer limited by his time, place, and circumstances. He becomes a timeless force of the cosmic Self. Timeless leaders like Christ and Krishna bear witness to their own magnificence as they resurrect from the flesh to the spirit. The nucleus of timeless leadership is not the shadowy ego that makes us believe that we are merely skin-clad entities. The core of timeless leadership is the liberated and Supreme soul Self that connects the trickle of our little lives to the abundant stream of Life.

# SUTRA 15

# TIMELESS LEADERS DISCOVER THEIR INVISIBLE SOURCE

## The Tree of Life

Krishna unveils before Arjuna the timeless code of human nature in both its manifest and unmanifest forms. He describes the journey of human life with the help of an inverted tree that has its roots above and its branches below. The roots point toward the invisible causal forces that create the field of manifestation of human nature like the leaves and branches of a tree. The physical form of a human being and all that he or she does in the material universe comes from the workshop of the invisible. Timeless leaders see that behind the perishable forms of Nature there is the imperishable unity of life that sustains Nature. The tree of life that Krishna talks about is sustained by the evolutionary energy of Nature that moves through the roots and feeds the trunk, the branches, and the leaves of the tree. This energy comes from the Self, which unites all of life in an integrated web of being.

## THE TREE OF LIFE

Krishna said to Arjuna that the one who grasps this timeless secret will become enlightened and fulfil his mission of life:

> The imperishable tree of life has its roots above, its branches below, and its leaves are its expressions of knowledge. Those who know this, know the whole truth.
>
> *(15.1)*

The tree of life that Krishna depicts to Arjuna is a reversal of the tree that we see with our ordinary senses. How often do we think of the roots of a tree when we see one by the roadside? Yet the roots hold in place the trunk, the branches, and the leaves of the tree. The roots are the cause that produces the effect that our eyes see as a tree. Krishna points out that our sensory world is a topsy-turvy world of perception where we are so obsessed with the effect that we do not investigate the cause.

The tree of life represents the diverse field of manifest as well as unmanifest life. Krishna describes the whole phenomenon of life as an interplay of matter, energy, and mind. The tree of life is rooted in the invisible being from which all of life derives its nourishment, much like roots that derive the nourishing sap from the soil and circulate it through all the branches of the tree. The leaves and the branches represent the varieties of life's expressions. Just as the varieties of leaves help us distinguish one tree from another, likewise many expressions of life forms from one life source help us learn about the many nuances of life. The many leaves thus represent many facets of the knowledge of life. We study physics, chemistry, zoology, physiology, botany, and psychology and make inferences on many facets of human life. Such inferences help us discover the laws of life in all its subtlety.

The tree of life is the timeless code of human nature both in its manifest and unmanifest form. The variety of facets of human nature—aggressive, narcissistic, passive, reflective—all sprout from the combination of three primary forces of Nature: inertia, dynamism, and illumination. Krishna elaborates on this timeless code as he instructs Arjuna:

> The branches of the tree of life are nourished by the forces of Nature, sense objects are its buds, the diffused roots of this tree stretch themselves to bind men to action.
>
> *(15.2)*

The tree of life has no stability. It changes its patterns and appearances faster than the human mind can grasp. The leaves of this tree multiply like many desires. These desires chase sense objects and indulge in repeated actions. Actions repeated form habits that bind a human being to his world. When the life in a human being is driven by personal will and habits of self-aggrandizement, he isolates himself by his petty desires and forfeits his access to the wholeness of life. An unenlightened leader's petty ego fragments the wholeness of life like a solitary leaf that flutters desolately on a tree in winter. Like that leaf, the leader longs to return again to the unity of life. Very soon a leader's life is carried away like the fragrance of a flower is carried away by a passing breeze.

Then Krishna exhorts Arjuna to acquire the essential knowledge of the tree of life. This knowledge cannot be acquired in the manner that one acquires the knowledge of the world by reading history, geography, or anatomy. The knowledge of the tree of life cannot come by gathering more information—it can come only by removing false notions that we have acquired about our life. These false notions come from attachment to sense-based data about our world. With our sense of sight we can count the number of seeds inside an apple; but we cannot count the infinite number of apples that can come from a single seed. So, Krishna says:

> In this mortal world the essence of the tree cannot be known. Neither can one know about its beginning or its end or its strength. Cut down this deep-rooted tree with the sharp axe of detachment. Then you can find the path of timeless life.
>
> *(15.3–4)*

The only discipline that will help a leader discover the unity of life is the discipline of detachment from obsessive pursuit of the senses. Such pursuits fragment and destroy the unity of life. The quest of a timeless leader is to go to the very source where life is one indivisible whole:

> A leader asked the enlightened Master, "All these stars, the whirling planets, the mountains, the rivers, and the trees—where do they come from?"
>     The Master whispered: "Where does your question come from?"

The discipline of detachment inculcates in the leader a purity of mind and the skill of genuine enquiry to explore truth that lies beyond the evidence of the senses. The leader realizes through enquiry that all creations of Nature, including the human form, are just effects and not the cause. The evidence that the effects exist makes it clear that a cause behind the effect exists. The fact that eyes can see and ears can hear is evident to us. What is not evident is that causal intelligence that enables the eyes to see and ears to hear. Krishna now presents the evidence that it is the invisible Self that is the cause of the tree of life:

> Using the mind, ears, eyes, nose, and the senses of taste and touch, the Self enjoys sense objects.
>
> *(15.9)*

The unconditioned consciousness inherent in the Self oozes out through the senses toward the path of our desires. This is how the leaves and branches of the tree of life sprout. As this consciousness travels further from the center of our Self the human form breaks away from the indivisible unity of life that characterises the Self. Then, a human being gets rooted in addictions of the material world, such as name, fame, and power. He thus gains the world but loses his soul. A timeless leader has to cut asunder and detach himself from the roots of addictive material attachments. Only then can he reclaim the magnificence of his invisible Self.

## THE INVISIBLE LEADER

The most significant role of a leader is to make the invisible clearly visible. Inspiration is invisible but inspired action is visible. Trust is invisible but trustworthy behaviour is visible. A leader has to constantly cross the bridge between what is unseen and that which is seen in order to connect with his followers.

The physical form of a human being and all that he does in the material universe comes from the workshop of the invisible. The visible physical shape of the human body is held together by an invisible skeletal and muscular structure. The muscular structure is in turn activated by invisible nerves.

The nerves on their part obey the command of the invisible mind. The mind follows the invisible intellect. The intellect is guided by the most invisible Self. With a powerful metaphor Krishna describes to Arjuna the invisible potential of the Self:

> When the supreme Self, the Lord of the Universe, enters a body or leaves it, He gathers these senses together and travels on with them, as the wind gathers fragrance while passing through the flowers.
>
> *(15.8)*

The invisible Self that Krishna is describing does not stay far away from us—it is just that we stray far away from it by chasing the outbound world of the senses. When we close our eyes we can't see our body, yet we can experience the stream of life that throbs through our veins and leaves its footprints in every heartbeat. Who is it that set in motion our first heartbeat? Who taught us to take our first breath? To find answers to these questions we have to look behind our finite frame in search of the infinite. Even if we trace the ancestry of our finite body to just ten generations before us, we will see a few million human bodies that have co-created us. Knowing this, the fine line between our finite bodies and the infinite course of life will be blurred.

Timeless leaders know that human life is like a river, the source and endpoint of which are both invisible. The human body is just a conduit as an electric bulb is a device for the passage of invisible electricity. Electricity is not designed for the bulb. Rather, the bulb is designed to obey the laws of electricity. When a narcissistic leader obsessively thinks about his physical appearance and his image in the organization, he becomes like a bulb devoid of the power of electricity. He is cut off from the unseen Self and the divine source that has created him. A wit once said that the difference between a god and a narcissist is only this: The god does not believe that he is a narcissist!

Leaders who celebrate their separateness and exclusivity from the rest are seen as successful models of leadership. Statues are erected for tyrants and despots. Yet their glory and fame are temporal and short-lived. If leaders identify themselves with their puny ego, they succeed in perpetuating the web of illusion for a while. Their power comes from the clamour of greedy followers and the glamour of the senses. Yet this power is as vulnerable to mortality as a dewdrop before a blazing sun. Timeless leaders, however, derive their power from unselfish service rather than servility to their ego's demands. Unselfish service frees the hold of the ego on the Self.

Here is a story that tells us that it is the spirit of service that is behind extraordinary achievements rather than the ego's need for approval:

> The master woodcarver was about to finish carving what looked like an exquisite statue. All those who saw the statue marveled, for it looked like the work of the spirits. When the Emperor of the land saw it, he asked, "What sort of talent is yours that can make such an extraordinary work of art?"
>
> The woodcarver said, "Almighty, I am just an ordinary workman. I am no genius. This is what I do before I carve a statue. First, I meditate for a week to calm my mind. When my mind is calm, I think no more about the rewards or emoluments that I may get by selling the statue. I just get absorbed in the work in progress. While at work I no longer think of praise or censure. Deeper into my work I forget my limbs and my whole body. I lose consciousness of the people surrounding me watching my work. Only my craft remains. In that state I walk into the forest and I intensely look at each tree until I find the one tree that is ready to become the statue in all its perfection. Then my hands start the work of carving. Setting my ego aside, nature meets nature in the work that is performed through me. This is the reason that when you look at the exquisite statue you call it the work of the spirit."

## FROM THE PERISHABLE TO THE IMPERISHABLE: QUEST FOR THE SUPREME SELF

Timeless leaders see that behind the perishable forms of Nature there is the imperishable unity of life that sustains Nature. The tree of life that Krishna talks about is sustained by the evolutionary energy of Nature that moves through the roots and feeds the trunk, the branches, and the leaves of the tree. This is the energy of the Self that unites all of life in an integrated web of being.

The deluded human mind that is shallow in its perception sees only the surface level of nature. On the surface Nature appears diverse and fragmented. This is because the mind that perceives this appearance is unable to see the underlying unity behind the fragmentation. The gross mind cannot see the subtle Self that unites everything. Krishna says,

> The deluded do not see the Self when it leaves the body or when it dwells within it.
>
> They do not see the Self enjoying sense objects or acting through the forces of Nature.
>
> Only those who have the eye of wisdom see.
>
> *(15.10)*

If we examine the composition of the ordinary, gross mind, we see that it is an unruly mob of thoughts and a swirl of moods. It is difficult to perceive the imperishable unity of life through such an instrument. Until the mind is calm it cannot quite reflect the unity of life. Just as a lake rippling with water distorts the reflection of the Moon, the waves of thoughts and emotions in a turbulent mind fragment the unity of life.

When the mind becomes meditative the number of thoughts inside it becomes less and less. With the receding wave of thoughts, such a mind becomes like the placid surface of a lake without waves. A meditative mind is then able to reflect the unity of life without distortion or fragmentation. We see the world of form and phenomena like a spectacle in a mirror. The images carried through the retina of the eyes fall on the mirror of the mind. If the mirror of the mind is not clear, all we see is a caricature of the spectacle of life.

When leaders behave like demigods, when they grandstand and intimidate others through fear and exclusion, they are just like caricatures of life's real face. When the same leaders see their actions in the mirror of the timeless they understand their follies. Such leaders see through their illusions. To be completely disillusioned with the illusions of the senses is the first step toward returning to the unity of life.

Krishna tells Arjuna that everything that is created in Nature and all that is manmade is perishable. Everything in Nature that a human being has converted into a resource—coal, oil, water, air—will perish and be exhausted. Even when one person exploits another as a "human resource" such exploitation will exhaust and diminish human capability. In making slaves of others we turn ourselves into slaves to our ego. The only imperishable aspect in us is our being, as Krishna reminds us:

> There are two aspects in Nature: the perishable and the imperishable. The perishable are creatures of the world; the imperishable is the changeless being.
>
> *(15.16)*

What isolates leaders from the tree of life is their inability to connect with their own being. This being is our changeless Self—it is the spirit that unites all the matter and all the elements of our universe into a harmonious whole. When leaders integrate themselves with their being they can experience their wholeness and their timeless, infinite spirit. Since we are spiritual beings living the illusion of the finite human form, nothing less than the infinite can fulfil us.

# LEADERS NEGOTIATE THE CROSSROADS

## The Divine and the Devilish

Arjuna is given an understanding of the crossroads of leadership: the divine and the devilish as two sides of human consciousness. Krishna provides Arjuna with a graphic description of the journey of a devilish leader through the path of despair and darkness. Krishna is not a speculative doomsday expert. He reminds Arjuna in no uncertain terms how the devilish path leads to bondage to the consequences of our thoughts and actions. He also proceeds to chart out the divine path that leads to freedom and light. Finally, Krishna assures Arjuna that he is born with divine attributes that lurk in all of us like light behind dark clouds.

## THE CROSSROADS OF LEADERSHIP: THE DIVINE AND THE DEVILISH

Krishna talks to Arjuna about the two paths that a leader can pursue. He also states that each of these paths leads to its own consequences:

> The divine qualities in a human being lead to freedom; the devilish to bondage.
>
> *(16.5)*

Here are two examples where leaders negotiated the crossroads in their lives:

After independence, South Africa was at the crossroads of the divine and the devilish. Leaders like Nelson Mandela and his people, who suffered brutal atrocities at the hands of a racist South African regime, had the option either to seek revenge or to pursue the path of forgiveness. One leader demanded the devilish capacity for evil and the other a divine capacity for good. Mandela chose the latter. Under his stewardship, South Africa scripted before the world a remarkable story of transition and transfer of power without massacre and bloodshed.

On September 29, 1982, Johnson & Johnson ( J&J), manufacturer of the analgesic drug Tylenol, was faced with a crisis. One after another, seven people in the Chicago area who had consumed Tylenol had died. Evidently, some miscreant had poisoned the Tylenol capsules with cyanide. Company CEO Jim Burke was at a crossroads: whether to pull from drugstores the entire production lot of more than $100 million in sales, or wash his hands of the whole thing and carry on with business as usual.

Under the leadership of Jim Burke, J&J distributed warnings to hospitals and distributors and halted Tylenol production and advertising. On October 5, 1982, it issued a nationwide recall of Tylenol products; an estimated 31 million bottles were in circulation with a retail value of over $100 million. The media complimented the company for being honest with its customers. While at the time of the crisis the company's market share collapsed from 35 percent to 8 percent, it rebounded in about a year and its profits multiplied manifold in a few years. Analysts who had virtually predicted the demise of the brand Tylenol and the company were quick to credit the J&J turnaround to the company's honest and transparent handling of the crisis.

Burke said that he really had no option but to pull the product, as such a choice would be consistent with the stated values of J&J. He also believed that when the company cared for the customer in a deeply spiritual way, the profits would take care of themselves.

The decisions that the two leaders made at their most defining moments of crisis were based on their values. The word *value* defines the intrinsic nature of whatever we value. Thus, being forgiving (as in the case of Mandela) or being truthful (as in Jim Burke's case) is valuable to these leaders not because someone told them that these virtues are valuable, but because they have realized in practice the value of these two virtues.

Krishna advocates self-restraint and compassion for others as virtues of the divine and cites self-indulgence and callousness as vices of the devilish. It is clear, therefore, that the divine and devilish are not so much societal codes as they are two states of consciousness. The human personality is a process of unfolding of the consciousness. A personality becomes divine by expanding the light of consciousness to include others as extensions of the Self. The same personality can become devilish by shrinking this light down to the dark center of the ego and its many appetites.

What Krishna describes as the divine is nothing but the journey to the core of light and illumination that is our source

Self. The devilish is a movement away from this source of light to the realms of darkness. Krishna attributes devilish behaviour to the ignorance of a leader about who he actually is. The devilish do things that they should avoid doing and avoid doing things that should be done because of this ignorance:

> People who have qualities belonging to the devil do not know what is to be done and what is to be abstained from.
>
> *(16.8)*

It is because of their basic ignorance about their source Self, which is the foundation of their faith, that the devilish are led astray. Just as they cannot stand firm on their Self belief, the devilish fall for any belief system that promises some crumbs of pleasure. The capacity to know what is the right action comes from discrimination. This discrimination is a quality of the source Self. The further one moves away from the Self the less discrimination one has:

> The demonic are unable to discriminate between the real and the unreal. As a result they hold distorted views on everything. They engage in action that leads to destruction.
>
> *(16.9)*

The consequence of lack of discrimination is programmed thinking. Krishna describes such programmed thinking in the language of possessiveness in which the devilish speak:

> "This I have gained today; tomorrow I will gratify another desire," they say. "This wealth is mine now and the rest will be mine before long."
>
> *(16.15)*

The consciousness of the devilish is stuck in the shallow sensory plane. Since they do not believe in the worth of their intrinsic Self, their belief is guided by the sensory chant: "More is the mission." The pursuit of more leads devilish leaders to thrust themselves ahead of all their followers in aggrandizing power and privileges:

> Giving themselves up to insatiable passions, hypocritical, deluded, and arrogant, they pursue only their personal ambitions.
>
> *(16.10)*

For the devilish, the entire journey of life is reduced to this equation:

$$\text{My body and its appetites} = \text{My life}$$

This puts devilish leaders on a collision course with the entire evolutionary journey of life. The evolution of life is not about success of the body. It is about the perfection of the species toward an ever-expanding consciousness. Once this basic truth about life is ignored our mind gets fragmented between what we are and what we assume ourselves to be. This fragmentation makes us fragile and leads us through the snare of personal desires to our ultimate demise:

> Perplexed by their fragmented mind, entangled in the snare of desires, infatuated, they sink into the horrors of hell.
>
> *(16.16)*

This is Krishna's graphic description of the journey of a devilish leader through the path of despair and darkness. Krishna is no speculative doomsday expert. He reminds Arjuna in no uncertain terms how the devilish path leads to bondage—the devilish binds us to the consequences of our thoughts and actions. He also proceeds to chart out the divine path that leads to freedom and light. Finally, Krishna assures

Arjuna that, like most human beings, he is born with the divine attributes that lurk in us like light behind dark clouds.

## TOXIC LEADERSHIP

Barbara Kellerman, who teaches leadership at the Kennedy School of Government at Harvard University, defines seven types of what she calls bad leadership. The first three types represent ineffective leadership:

1. Incompetent
2. Rigid
3. Intemperate

Incompetence is characterized by a leader and his followers who lack the will or skill to sustain effective action. In rigidity, the leader and his followers are unwilling to accept any new ideas or adapt to change. Intemperate represents the leader's and his followers' lack of self-control.

The next four types represent unethical leadership:

4. Callous
5. Corrupt
6. Insular
7. Evil

Callousness comes from an uncaring or an unkind attitude toward people. Corrupt leaders and their followers are given to deception, stealing, or cheating. Insular leaders disregard the welfare of their followers. Evil leaders like Gaddafi commit atrocities and use pain and genocide as instruments of power.

We have a whole spectrum representing the dark shades of leadership, including Hitler, Colonel Gaddafi, and, from the corporate world, former Enron CEO, Jeffery Skilling, and Martha

Stewart. To talk about good leadership without reference to toxic leadership would be the same as talking about a fulfilling lunch without reference to the pangs of hunger, or the search for a perfect medical cure without reference to the disease.

Dr. Kellerman raises two important questions about the existing body of literature on leadership:

1. Can *leadership* always be synonymous with *good leadership*?
2. Why are we afraid to acknowledge, much less admit, the dark side of leadership?

To find the answers to these questions, we have to go deep into the average human mind, which cannot see the connection between the cause and effect of toxic leadership. The cause of toxicity in leadership arises from a leader's primary ignorance. There are three foundational flaws in the assumptions of leadership that have become toxic:

1. Life is just the physical expression of itself.
2. The meaning of life is nothing more than the sensations of the body.
3. There are no consequences of ego-based actions because one cannot physically see them.

Eknath Easwaran, one of India's most respected spiritual teachers, explains that the reason leaders themselves cannot experience the consequence of their devilish actions is simply the fact that it takes a long time before the consequences of toxic leadership show up. The destruction of our ecosystem, the depletion of the ozone layer of our atmosphere, the melting of the polar icecaps, and the contamination of Earth's water resources are slowly showing up as the consequences of callous, intemperate, and corrupt leadership over the past few centuries.

The two forces of industrial civilization—speed and greed—have created for us an illusion of accomplishment. We superimpose on the human world the restless dynamism of the mechanical universe. Someone riding a superfast bullet train is bound to experience a certain sense of dynamism and power. Yet the ruthless dynamism is an attribute of the train and not of the person who is riding it. Like the speeding train, the onward push of our desires creates in us a sense of being alive. Yet, this constant proliferation of desires and the fast-paced craving for their fulfilment take us away from our core purpose.

Our business keeps us busy, yet we rarely ask, "Busy for what purpose?" The ego and its unchecked desires do not ask such questions. Yet the ego's onward and forward movement to stand ahead of others leaves behind a trail of consequences. Just as the firing of a rifle causes a recoil at the very source from where the rifle was fired, the ego's forward impetus leaves behind its toxic residue in the mind of the leader who has marched ahead. Unlike gunfire, however, the time-lag between cause and effect of the ego's movement is too great for us to notice it. But consequences are bound to show up in the foreseeable future. Each generation reaps the crops of sorrow that its predecessors have sown.

## THE RETURN JOURNEY

Krishna lays down the milestones along a leader's return journey from Self-forgetfulness and delusion and their consequent darkness back to life and light:

> Fearlessness, purity of mind and heart, steadfastness in knowledge, charity, self-restraint, sacrifice, self-study, austerity and uprightness, absence of anger, truth, harmlessness, compassion toward all, courtesy, modesty, valour, forgiveness, fortitude, freedom from hate and vanity—these are qualities of those who take the divine path.
>
> *(16.1–3)*

This is much more than a laundry-list of virtues that constitute the moral code of good leaders. In fact, this is neither a moral nor a social code. If anything, this is a code for two great movements of life: the exterior and the interior. The tree of life that Krishna described earlier is an expression of the exterior movement of life. It is the movement of expression, acquisition, and ambition to the extremities of the world. There is at the same time a countermovement, the return journey, toward the internal, toward compassion and peace, toward the core of our being. Every Age, every cycle of human evolution integrates these two movements of human nature. The following story illustrates this:

The warrior had come to the Master seeking peace and wisdom.

He urged the Master: "Tell me, how do I attain wisdom and peace? I am a warrior and I will not go back until I achieve my goals. To begin with, can you teach me how to differentiate between the divine and the devilish?"

The Master eyed the warrior and said in a mocking tone of voice, "You are a dumb-headed fellow. How will you ever attain wisdom with your dull wit?"

The warrior's pride was hurt and he was seething in anger as he pulled out his sword and was about to chop off the head of the sage.

The sage made eye contact with the warrior and said, "This anger of yours and the action that you are about to commit under its sway is devilish."

The warrior now understood that the sage had taught him the lesson he was looking for. He dropped his sword and asked for the sage's forgiveness for his misplaced anger.

"Wait a minute," the sage said to the warrior. "This state of consciousness that you are in now is what you may call divine. Lesson over. You may now return to your practice!"

# LEADERS FOLLOW THEIR FAITH

## The Journey of Self-Giving

Arjuna quizzes Krishna on the nature of faith and its relationship with the real world. Krishna answers by saying that in the human constitution, faith is the *deep structure* of not just our purest spiritual quests but also our worldly passions and our blind prejudices. Faith embraces the whole range of our beliefs and behaviours from the mystical to the mundane. Krishna counsels Arjuna on three kinds of faith based on three types of human nature: *slothful*, *dynamic*, and *illumined*. From slothful inertia to dynamism and then onto illumination is the story of the evolution of the human mind. The three kinds of faith that Krishna alludes to play out in the daily lives of leaders. They show up in the kinds of work leaders engage in, the food they like, the way they speak, and the gifts they give.

Finally, Krishna talks about Self-reliance as the greatest gift that a leader can give to a follower.

## FAITH: THE DEEP STRUCTURE OF LEADERSHIP

Arjuna asks Krishna, "What is faith? Is it purity, passion, or sheer ignorance?" Krishna answers that faith is inherent in the human heart. Faith is the deepest driving force that shapes a human being's values and beliefs. It is faith that shapes one's destiny:

> The faith of every human is according to his nature. By nature he is full of faith. A man is in fact what his faith makes him.
>
> *(17.3)*

Let us take the example of two corporate leaders from different parts of the world who build successful business empires based on their faith.

William Wrigley Jr., who built a fortune in early twentieth-century America selling Wrigley's gum, discovered something about adhering to one's faith. He understood that a salesman's greatest strength is to be able to keep to his faith. He knew that almost all potential buyers will say "No" at first. The art of salesmanship is holding onto one's faith in the product until the buyer has exhausted his last "No."

Narayana Murthy, the iconic founder and CEO of the Indian IT company Infosys Technologies, talks about his faith in data. As a trained engineer he places his faith in facts. He says, "When we make a decision we do so based on the facts on the table. No one can argue with hard facts. In God we trust; everybody else brings data to the table."

These two different companies grew their respective business cultures based on what their leaders implicitly believed in. Just as a tree shoots up toward the sky based on the depth and vitality of its roots, a human being attains the heights of accomplishment based on the kind of faith he or she is endowed with. It is the momentum of faith that gives the dynamism and direction to a leader's work in the world.

When he has deep faith in some ideal or course of work, the leader becomes fairly autonomous. He rarely needs an endorsement from the outside world when his faith has become truly abiding. Gandhi's faith in nonviolence was like this:

> For me non-violence is a creed. I must act up to it whether I am alone or have companions.
>
> But non-violence, which is a quality of the heart, cannot come by an appeal to the brain.
>
> *(Mohandas Gandhi, "Both Happy and Unhappy,"*
> Harijan, *June 29, 1940)*

Faith defines the critical decisions in a leader's life because his heart is where his faith is. Faith is a decision of the heart. It is, therefore, the most powerful dynamo in human achievement. The Bible endorses this: *As [a man] thinketh in his heart, so is he* (Proverbs 23:7). The internal governing structure of a leader's decision and action thus comes from his heart. The heart is the deep structure where a leader's hopes, fears, thoughts, and emotions reside.

## THREE KINDS OF FAITH

The human heart finds whatever it truly places its faith in:

> The sons of two kings of ancient India, Yudhisthir and Duryadhana, had two different kinds of faith. Yudhisthir lived by the values of purity of speech and goodness. Duryadhana was cunning and devilish at heart. Their teachers designed a test to assess what the two could accomplish by their faith.

The teacher called for Duryadhana early in the morning and asked him go around the entire kingdom and count the number of good people that he could find until sunset.

Then the teacher called Yudhisthir and asked him to go around the kingdom and search for and count all the really evil people that he could possibly spot before sunset.

As the sun was about to set that evening, Duryadhana, whose heart had faith in the devil, returned empty handed as he was unable to spot a single good man in the entire kingdom.

Soon thereafter, Yudhisthir, whose heart had faith in the goodness of man, also returned without any success, because he could not find a single evil man or woman in the entire kingdom.

Just as Yudhisthir sees a world of good based on his faith, Duryadhan's faith in evil makes see him see nothing but evil.

In counselling Arjuna on the three kinds of faith based on the evolution of the three types of human nature (slothful, dynamic, and illumined), Krishna describes the nature of this evolution as austerity of the human mind:

> Serenity, good-hearted silence, self-control, purity of nature—
> these together are called austerities of the mind.
>
> *(17.16)*

Amadeo Peter Giannini started his career in the early twentieth century as a vegetable broker and later founded the Bank of America. He pioneered branch banking and Bank of America became the largest bank in the world during his lifetime. Giannini had a characteristic austerity of the mind: He would give away in charity to orphanages and medical and educational institutions large amounts of money when-ever his personal wealth came close to the one-million-dollar mark. When Giannini died in 1949, the combined assets of

Bank of America and Transamerica were more than $7 billion. Yet, A.P. Giannini succeeded in his personal goal of never becoming a millionaire.

We can see from this example that austerity of mind is not just a mystical pursuit. One can be in the thick of the material world and still practice austerity to good effect. Such austerity gives the leader a vision beyond ordinary perception. An austere mind is able to rise from dullness to dynamism and then onto deep reflection. When it came to problem solving, Gianinni had a unique method that he described in terms of the mind's movement:

> In working out any plan or idea, I use what you might call the intermittent method. I hit the problem hard, then leave it for a while, and later come back. This method permits me to bring to the particular problem many ideas that come from mature reflection.
>
> *(Julie M. Fenster,* In the Words of Great Business Leaders, *John Wiley & Sons, New York, 2000, p. 221)*

The three kinds of faith that Krishna alludes to show up in various ways in the leader's daily life. Taking just the habit of speech, notice how the forces of inertia, dynamism, and illumination enact themselves in the way a leader speaks:

**1.** The least evolved way of speaking is to speak lies. This is when the speaker is steeped in inertia. Many leaders speak without verifying facts. Many others deliberately tell lies to cover their mistakes or prevent trouble for themselves. When a lie is spoken knowingly, there is internal disharmony between the "knower" and the "speaker." In the case of habitual lying, the knower is divorced from the speaker to such an extent that the person begins to inhabit a make-believe world fabricated out of lies. Very soon such a world collapses around this type of leader when reality bites back.

2. The second kind of speech is dynamic. It evokes passions in the listener. Some leaders place their faith in the type of speech that sometimes generates hatred and adversarial emotions. Many motivational leaders in corporations raise battle cries of "killing the competition" and "scorching the market" and "head-hunting." When the company is in rapid expansion mode, leaders often look for managers in whom the aggressive dynamism they seek is manifest. But the trouble starts when such aggression runs against the enterprise itself. What happens when a speech-inflamed colleague imposes his high-testosterone-driven moods on his hapless teammates?

3. The third and the most evolved kind of speech according to Krishna is the one in which the leader is illumined. This kind of speech is of the most refined variety, born of great mental discipline:

> Speaking words that are truthful, pleasing, and beneficial—this is austerity of speech.
>
> *(17.15)*

Before he acquires the gift of his illumined speech, the leader has to go through three kinds of mental austerities, in a manner similar to the security checks that the air traveller has to undergo. The first check comes from the security officer, who says: "You can go ahead with your speech, provided it is truthful." If it is not truthful, the speech is best not allowed to go. The second security officer says, "It is truthful all right, but is it pleasant? If it is truthful but unpleasant, it's best you go back!" The third and final security question is, "It is both truthful and pleasant, but is it beneficial to the one you are speaking to? If it is not beneficial, you cannot let it go." The speech that successfully clears these three austerity checks is the most evolved and the most impactful.


## THE ART AND SCIENCE OF SELF-GIVING

In the corporate world giving (charity) is synonymous with possession of wealth. In truth, it is the faith behind giving that makes one rich and not how much wealth one possesses. Giving is much more than money laundering or merit mongering. True giving is about returning to the unity of life wherein the giver and the receiver fulfil each other as the two halves of a whole process. How could a company manufacture a million units of their product if there were no customers to buy them? For each committed giver, there must be an equally intentional receiver. Krishna cautions Arjuna:

> Whatever is done without faith, whether it is sacrifice, austerity, or gift, is unreal. Such actions, Arjuna, have no real significance either here or hereafter.
>
> *(17.28)*

Krishna goes on to classify three kinds of gifts. The first comes from an illumined mind. It is a gift given without thought of return on investment. It is given at the proper time and circumstances and to a worthy person. Such a gift is pure and serves the purpose of the whole. The second kind comes from a mind that is dynamic—passionate but not illumined. This gift is given (often grudgingly) with an expectation of the results it will produce for the giver—whether it is name or fame or material benefits. The third kind of gift comes from an ignorant mind dominated by inertia. This giving happens at an inappropriate time, under unsuitable circumstances, and to an unworthy person. This gift of ignorance is often given with disrespect or contempt.

The true gift is not the gift of possessions but the gift of the Self. The first step in the art of Self-giving is to break down the ego barrier that prompts the leader to think: "I, the body, am the giver." This is an expression of ego-promoting arrogance that taints the gift at its source. When a gift is given from the ego rather than from the source Self such a gift fragments the whole cycle of giving and taking. The greater the claim that the giver makes about his giving, the smaller the cycle of giving becomes and the deeper his ignorance is. The wealth of the giver, even if he is a billionaire, comes from many sources of contribution. He therefore cannot legitimately claim to be the sole giver.

The art of giving, as Krishna reminds us, comes with context sensitivity. The leader who gives something to a follower, whether praise, power, or promotion, has to be sensitive to the context in which such gifts are given. Praise or promotion given when they are not deserved creates a swollen ego in the receiver as well as a loss of morale in the ranks of others who are denied such privileges. Krishna rightly points out that no one really gains when gifts are out of context. In the worst-case scenario these gifts turn out to be utterly useless, like a bald man receiving the gift of a fine tortoise-shell comb!

The purest gift that a leader can give to a follower is the gift of Self-reliance. Krishna is a Self-realized individual, complete unto himself. Yet, he comes down to the field of battle to bring Arjuna up from despair and make him Self-reliant. Self-reliance is nothing but faith in the larger Self beyond one's physical body and ego. Creators of immense material wealth, like A.P. Giannini, have found that the discipline of thrift is much more difficult to practice than the art of being profligate. Giannini discovered that he could actually give the gift of thrift and Self-reliance to the generations that would follow him:

> My hardest job has been to keep from being a millionaire.
> Personally, I have never been able to understand the passion

for storing up a great fortune. Wealth is a hard master, imposing many burdens, worries, fears, and distractions. They say it's for their children. That's bunk. The worst thing that can happen to a boy is to be barred from the right to work and struggle and make his own way.

*(George Creel, "My Hardest Job Is to Keep from Being a Millionaire,"* The American Magazine, *January 1931, p. 25, as quoted in Julie M. Fenster,* In the Words of Great Business Leaders, *John Wiley & Sons, New York, 2000)*

# LEADERSHIP IS TRANSCENDENCE

## The Unity of Two Wills

In this final sutra, Krishna tells Arjuna how the tentative fighter can finally be transformed into a resolute warrior. Whereas the fighter seeks success, the warrior pursues perfection that sustains success. Success is a temporary state, whereas the quest for perfection is timeless. Krishna shows how the threefold paths of leadership—knowledge, action, and devotion—become one in the pursuit of perfection. The journey of perfection is nothing but our evolutionary urge to transcend the limitations of our physical and mental condition. Transcendence is the ultimate goal of such a quest. *Transcendence* is the merging of personal will with the impersonal will of the cosmic order. That is how a leader like Arjuna moves from the temporal to the timeless. He becomes an instrument of the spontaneous source of all creation: the timeless order and harmony of the universe that guides our thoughts, feelings, and actions. In the path of transcendence the will of the human unites with the will of the divine. The will of Arjuna merges with the will of Krishna. When this happens, victory, success, prosperity, and righteous order are sure to follow.

## THE SOURCE AND RESOURCE

In leadership, the first step represents the whole journey. It's like the first impression becoming the most enduring one in a social interaction. How does this happen? The first step sets the direction for all the other steps that follow. Imagine what happens when the first button in your shirt is wrongly buttoned! All the other buttons are bound to be wrongly aligned. Leadership is about setting the right direction. This is the first step, from which the rest of the steps naturally follow.

How does someone like Arjuna, who is learning the ropes in leadership, know which is the first step? Krishna, the timeless leader, teaches him the secret: The first step is to surrender the entire spectrum of our energy—physical, psychological, and emotional—to our spiritual source. Why is this so? The spiritual source is the cause and we are the effects of that cause. The spirit in us is the *source*; the tangible material expressions of this spirit, such as our thoughts, actions, or emotions, represent the *resource*. Timeless leaders understand that whereas the spirit is the source, all of matter is the resource.

What happens when a leader like Arjuna surrenders to the spiritual source embodied by Krishna? In doing so, Arjuna is connected to his timeless spiritual potential. Source is the pure potentiality from which our thoughts, emotions, and actions originate. When you are a source the world exists in you. When you are a resource you exist in the world. Drop a pebble into a still pool of water. You can see ripples of water moving outward in circles. Do you know where the ripples finally end? If you observe carefully, you will see that the ripples finally come back to the center where the pebble hit the water.

The entire dynamism of the rippling water begins and ends with the point-source where the pebble first hit the water.

When the Earth moves around the Sun and comes back to its original place, it completes a *revolution*. All revolutions have one destiny: to come back to the source to discover a new reality there. The source is always the origin of creativity and pure potentiality. This is how leaders create revolutions: by revisiting and giving new expression to human potential. Great revolutions, like the French Revolution or the Industrial Revolution, are unique achievements of human civilization. In both these instances leaders tapped into those perennial seeds of the human source such as freedom and inventiveness, which blossomed into mass movements.

When a leader thinks, acts, or feels from a true source, whatever he sends out into the world comes back multiplied. The process is like a seed producing a whole forest. The seed is the source and the forest is the resource. The human source is the factor of creation. Whatever the source creates becomes a resource. Krishna says: "Arjuna, surrender all your resources—physical, psychological, and emotional—to your spiritual source, which I embody, and your powers will be magnified manifold." Krishna is merely restating an eternal law: The subtle source purifies and magnifies the gross resource. When a tree in the forest perishes it leaves behind the distilled essence of the tree in the form of a seed. The seed then becomes the source of a whole new forest by the law of pure potentiality.

To understand the relationship between a source and a resource take the example of a playwright who writes a play. The playwright is the source, and the script he writes is a resource. The various actors in the play are resources subject to the thoughts and imagination of the playwright—he can change any character and make the character do whatever he thinks is appropriate to serve the purpose of the play. This is the creative and transformational potential of the source: It can *transform a resource.*

When a leader expresses himself from the source of pure potential, as Krishna has done for Arjuna, he is able to transform his followers. The followers are released from their restrictive neural chemistry of fear and guilt, which makes them feel like small and isolated entities. A timeless leader enables followers to get out of their own restrictive thought processes and emotional maps. Leaders thus guide their followers back into the fullness of their pure potential. This works in the same manner as a magnet that transforms the potential of an iron bar and makes it magnetic. In this a timeless leader leads his followers to themselves—to their own magnetic magnificence!

I once noticed a young woman in Johannesburg, South Africa, who was serving in a Thai restaurant I happened to visit for lunch. The restaurant had just opened for customers. This young woman was standing in front of a mirror with a burning incense stick in her hand and a half-smile on her face. I asked her what she was doing in front of the mirror. She replied, "I am worshipping myself." I was amused then. Today, I realize that she was bowing down to this magnificent source inside of her in search of inspiration.

## THE ALGEBRA OF ATTACHMENT

"What is the source of your power?" asked the follower.

"My being in touch with the source," replied the leader.

"You are really connected to the source?" quizzed the follower.

"In truth, I am the source," replied the leader.

"That would be the height of arrogance," mocked the bewildered follower.

"No, it would be the height of arrogance if you were *not* in touch with the source. Everything in this universe comes from the source. If you are not the source, you are the ego. In the battle between your ego and the universe, your ego is bound to lose," said the leader.

Krishna now enables Arjuna to explore the process that blocks his realization of the source. We can define this process as the algebra of attachment. Algebra is a branch of mathematics that deals with the rules of operations in our world. Elementary algebra describes an operation as a combination of constants and variables. Attachment can be represented as the combination of our real and sourceful Self (constant) and our ego and its varied reactions and movements (variable). The never-changing source Self when conditioned by the forever-changing movements of the ego creates psychological attachment.

The egocentric mind creates its polarized points of attachment in what it likes and what it dislikes. The ego crafts its own story about the world it inhabits. The story is largely fictitious yet it seems real because the conditioned source Self is contributing to the story. Imagine you are flying in an airplane that is caught in turbulent weather. You are worried about the consequences of the plane crashing. As a passenger, you cannot do much about the bumpy flight, yet your mind is attached to the imagined consequences and you create many imaginary scenarios of a potential plane crash from 30,000 feet up. Your anxiety does not improve the quality of your flying experience. What improves it is the pilot's deft navigation. Ideally, you should leave the consequences of the flight experience to the pilot. You would do well to detach yourself from your worry.

Appropriating to the ego what belongs to the larger reality of Nature is the entire game of attachment. Going back to our flying example, the ego of the passenger falsely believes that "he is flying," whereas the truth is that it is the plane that is flying and is maneuvered by the pilot and the passenger is just sitting on a chair as he is being given a ride. But the ego collapses the whole reality into a false belief: "I am flying." Or take the simple statement of a man who has an upset stomach. He says from the center of the ego: "I am sick." In reality his stomach is fighting a bout of indigestion. He collapses this little physical ailment into an existential concern by saying "I am sick." This is a game that we constantly play with ourselves. When we are not attached to the source, our mind becomes addicted to whatever makes the ego perpetuate its story.

This identification with and attachment to the limited and temporary condition creates the illusion of personality. On the job, this kind of identification leads to workers getting stuck in their roles and job descriptions as though this was their whole reality. The accountant at work continues to behave like an accountant in the arena of his relationships at work. He tries to micromanage people in the same way he prepares a balance sheet. The leader's work is to lead the personality back to the broader amplitude of the human source. The leader, Krishna, teaches his follower, Arjuna, to discover their shared source through awareness.

Arjuna is in a dilemma. His ego's conversation goes something like this: "Will I succeed or not succeed in fighting this war with my own kin?" Arjuna is attached to the ego's psychological movement, which says, "I am fighting this whole war." The truth is that Arjuna has been mentally preparing for this war of redemption for years. His thoughts and emotions have built up a momentum that has generated a reaction within his own and from the opposition's camp. So Arjuna's mental condition is just one wave in a sea of thought and emotional energy that constitutes the war "atmosphere." But Arjuna's ego is appropriating the whole war to himself. His ego is saying, "I am worried as I am doing the war." Krishna is trying to bring him out of the delusion of *doership,* which is his ego usurping the larger field of awareness.

As with Arjuna, when our senses are attracted toward the energies in physical Nature, there is a movement or a response. It is in the very design and nature of living systems that this interaction goes on without our personal effort. When gravity pulls us downward we stand on the surface of the Earth. We are not *doing* the standing. The standing just happens by the natural cause-and-effect relationship between gravity and our physical mass. We are merely the field of awareness in which this interplay of our inner nature and the outer Nature goes on. We are not the doer or actor. The relationship between our senses and the world outside is the dynamic play of Nature. When we are attached to this play and call it "our action" we are deluded, like someone sitting inside a fast-moving train who wrongly thinks, "I am moving fast."

What would be the productive capacity of an organization wherein most employees were concerned with doing their work rather than with taking credit for their personal achievements? Such an organization would be a powerful engine of contribution. This is how timeless leaders transform people within organizations. They help followers detach their minds from egotistic pursuits and go about their business in pursuing a purpose beyond their own personal cravings. This is how great wars are won and great organizations take shape.

## RENUNCIATION AND REGENERATION OF THE LEADER

"What's the point of renunciation?" asked the follower.

The leader replied, "Just do this: Stretch your hand and hold this precious diamond on the open palm of your hand for as long as you can."

The follower did as instructed. But very soon the muscles in his outstretched hands started aching and he decided to put the diamond down on the floor.

The leader quietly said: "That's the point of renunciation—you cannot hold onto anything for too long without suffering the consequences."

Timeless leaders realize that renunciation is not merely about letting go; it is just as much about the regeneration of energy in a decaying system. Renunciation is like pruning a rose garden and weeding it so that the fresh blooms regenerate themselves. Without renouncing the old there is no regeneration of the new.

Renunciation is the process through which any system—physical or psychological—replenishes itself and avoids entropy. When one observes the cycle of seasons, one can see that dead leaves fall off a tree in winter and the tree regenerates in a burst of new foliage in spring. So the human mind renounces the rush of daytime activity to fall into the stillness of sleep at night so that the body can feel fresh the next morning.

What holds true for the outer Nature also holds true for our inner nature. When we are engaged in work, part of our mind has to remain in action mode. However, along with the active mind, what also gets switched on is the habitual ego-driven *speculative* mind, which conjures up such unnecessary thoughts as: "Will I or won't I succeed?" or "How can one succeed with colleagues who are perpetual jerks?" or "It is difficult to succeed in this country."Whenever a thought arises in the mind our ego catches hold of it and creates an imaginary narrative that does not serve us. In fact, the speculative mind depletes the capability of the active mind. Renunciation is thus the conscious intent to minimise the leakage of human energy through thoughtless speculation and mindless conjectures. When the light of our awareness is shed on such energy leakage, we stop speculating and get on with our work in the fullness of our capacity.

Krishna educates Arjuna on the art and practice of renunciation. In the contemporary context, here are three simple ways that renunciation can be performed:

1. Renouncing old habits (*sama*): Conscious restraint of the habitual flow of the mind toward sense objects—taking a break from the Internet, for instance.
2. Renouncing emotional outbursts (*ksanti*): To be patient and forgiving even when perceiving a small injustice done to yourself by another person. This means not

cursing when another driver cuts you off in violation of traffic laws.

3. Renouncing personal aggrandizement (*kartavya bhavana*): Not appropriating credit for what one has not actually done. Many corporate leaders are tempted to steal the limelight for what others have collectively accomplished. To give to others credit where it is due is the renunciation of doership.

When we give up not the action but the psychological wrinkles of anxiety and goal obsession, we regenerate our natural state of being. We feel automatically energized when our minds are established in their natural equanimity. The way to identify a regenerated leader is by her equanimity of mind, which is austere in thought and steady in action and therefore ultimately effective.

Our mental apparatus goes through a tug-of-war between speculation and action. Yet this tug-of-war can be reconciled: Those actions that are done with an unselfish motive for the welfare of others do not bind us to our speculating ego. This kind of action comes from the spiritual source and not from the ego-tainted mind.

## THE PATH OF TRANSCENDENCE

The leader drew the attention of the follower to a row of burning candles and asked: "Tell me, where was the fire before it came to the wick of the candle?"

"Simple," answered the follower, "it came from the match that struck the fire."

"Fair, yet where was the fire before it was struck on the matchstick?" persisted the leader.

"Well," mumbled the follower scratching his head, "somewhere in the chemical on the head of the matchstick."

"Good! But where was the fire before it found its way inside the chemicals that housed it?" the leader persisted.

The follower gave up.

The leader concluded, "In reality, fire is potentially present everywhere in our atmosphere. Fire emerges wherever the conditions for its emergence are met. All we need is to transcend our mental modes in order to discover that fire is really everywhere!"

Transcendence is the art and science of being real. How does one access reality? Reality unveils itself through the following steps:

$$Facts \rightarrow Truth \rightarrow Reality$$

Ordinarily we do not see reality. Through our senses we merely see facts. When we look at a tree we view only the fact of a tree: a green image with leaves and branches. But at the sensory level we do not see the "truth" of the whole tree. To see the truth of the tree we have to go beyond the evidence of our senses. We have to apply our mind and understand that what we see of the tree is not the whole tree. We have to transcend the evidence of the senses to perceive that the roots of the tree, which we cannot see, are also very much part of the reality of the tree. So facts belong to the senses. Truth belongs to the discriminating mind. But reality is even greater than that. Reality escapes the grasp of the mind.

The reality of the tree extends beyond the trunk and the roots. The real tree is greater than our mental conception of it. The real tree is integral to a whole ecosystem consisting of rains, soil, sunshine, and the air we breathe. In fact the real tree is not a tree at all—it is an assortment of energy systems of particles and waves that extend to the whole of the Cosmos. This can't be understood by our ordinary truth-seeking mind. We have to transcend the mind's structures to access reality, for reality does not yield its whole secret to the organized mind.

How does one achieve this transcendence? The first step is through non-identification with the data presented to us by the senses. Then second step is through nonattachment to the models created by the mind. Reality then quietly dawns on the open mind. The process is somewhat like going to sleep. We wrongly identify our *body* as going to sleep. Actually the body does not go to sleep—it simply lies down. Sleeps comes by itself to the body. The body does not create sleep. Similarly, reality comes by itself when we lay down the screen of our senses and the defensiveness of our minds. This is the whole journey of transcendence through which Krishna is guiding Arjuna.

Krishna started by challenging the data that Arjuna's senses presented as his rationale for not engaging in the righteous war. His limbs were trembling, his mouth was dry with fear, and his skin was burning. For Arjuna, all these sense-data items were symptoms of a breakdown of his resolve to fight. For Krishna, this was not a breakdown but the precursor to a breakthrough. Krishna understood that Arjuna's despondency was just a prelude to his evolution to a higher order of thinking, feeling, and action. Arjuna's mental models were breaking down. He was finding it difficult to reconcile himself to the fight he would have to have with his "kith and kin" in the rival camp and the consequences of the disruption of social order that the war would bring about. When a system—whether physical or psychological—evolves to a higher potential, there is bound to be disruption in the existing order of things and thoughts.

Krishna was keenly aware of this. The reality is that Krishna is Arjuna's own imperishable source Self. By a gradual process of transcendence of the sensory and then mental barriers, Krishna leads Arjuna to the ultimate reality of the source Self. It is here that the will of the follower and the will of the leader merge into the pursuit of the ultimate human purpose: the realization of the source Self.

Then Krishna proceeded to strike at Arjuna's organized mental defences against engaging in the war. He leads Arjuna from his delusional thoughts to the tranquillity of wisdom. He inspires Arjuna to rise from non-action to the freedom of spontaneous action. He instils in Arjuna the power to awaken from fantasy to deep devotion to the real goal of all wars: the realization of our larger identity—our source Self.

The human condition is a fascinating seek-and-find instrument. Like Arjuna, we find what we really seek. Arjuna seeks in the context of his time a solution to his vexing problem. Apparently, his problem is his inability to get up and fight. But in reality Arjuna is in a relentless hunt for his larger *I*—the true identity of the source Self that Krishna embodies.

Transcendence is the process of realizing the source Self as the pure observer. It is like the lens of a camera. The lens moves over flowers and filth; the lens surveys valleys and hills. The lens reflects whatever image falls on it. Yet the lens remains unaffected by whatever it reflects. Krishna is like the lens reflecting the pitfalls and potential of Arjuna without being in any way affected by them. When Arjuna realizes Krishna's vision, he sees what Krishna is able to see: reality untouched by the mind's reactions to it. Transcendence implies the ceasing of mental reactions like a lens ceases to react to what is projected on it.

In transcendence there is an awakening to a different kind of energy. It is the energy of the reflective—pure awareness not conditioned by thoughts. It is a higher-frequency energy uncontaminated by the movements of the judging, calculating, reactive mind. In this state the ego does not function as an interpreter or a storyteller: The ego simply falls silent. Imagine standing on the seashore before an ethereally beautiful sunset. For a fleeting few seconds the conscious mind transcends to an energy state where thoughts have ceased and "the breath is taken away" by a state of silence. In this silence Arjuna and Krishna—the human and the divine—come closest to one another.

# THE UNITY OF TWO WILLS: THE FIGHTER AND THE WARRIOR

An organization is not just an assembly of systems and structures but an alchemy of the collective wills of its people. When people within an organization perceive the system and structures—both social and psychological—as barriers to realizing their potential as source Self they become fighters. Like Arjuna, they see themselves as helpless resources fighting uphill battles against unjust systems. This goes on until a leader like Krishna comes along and makes them evolve from mundane fighters to true warriors.

Fighters fight with their swords and shields. They become victims of their binary minds: fight or flight; offence or defence. They see organizational structures and systems as physical barriers that they must overcome. Fighters depend on their limited physical and mental effort and their ego-propelled will. Fighters are doomed to fail like a fragile twig in a raging storm.

The true warrior does not travel the path of the divided and binary mind. Before he takes up the fight, the warrior first surrenders his will to the will of the source, which is the ultimate reality. He draws his arrow from the focal point of his source Self. Just as the fighter cannot win, the warrior cannot lose. His invincibility is that of a hollow branch through which the wind of inspiration passes. The raging storm of opposition becomes the melodious music of the flute as it passes through the hollow branch. By surrendering his will to the larger will of the source the warrior reclaims his omnipotence.

The unity of two wills happens when the light of awareness connects the human with the divine. It is the same light. When sunlight falls on a highly polished diamond the Sun is reflected in all its splendour. It is the receptivity of the diamond and its reflective capacity that determine how it will reflect the Sun. Arjuna represents human effort: the diligently cut diamond. Without light, even the best of diamonds would appear like a dull stone. Without the light of awareness that Krishna brings, Arjuna is like a dull stone. When he becomes aware and inspired by being in the company of Krishna, Arjuna is able to reflect the light of awareness that Krishna embodies. This is the unity of two wills: the will of the human and the will of the divine.

Arjuna is the seeker of Self-knowledge. Krishna is that deep-seated wisdom to which all seeking leads. It is the relationship that a thirsty man has with a fountain of water. Arjuna's thirst is quenched. The energy of knowledge merges into the energy of wisdom and understanding. Krishna urges: "Concentrate your mind on me and devote your whole heart to me. You have listened with deep attention to what I have said. But have you understood this teaching and accepted it as worthwhile? Has it dispelled your delusion?"

Krishna does not impose himself on Arjuna; he gives his follower a choice. Where there is choice, there is freedom. When one chooses to follow a leader from the foundation of freedom rather than from compulsion, that choice is likely to be more enduring.

Krishna finally says to Arjuna, "The one I love, I would set him free even from me." This is the final threshold that timeless leaders have to cross. The unenlightened leader binds the follower in the vicious cycle of insecurity, expectation, and dependence. The timeless leader gives the follower the freedom to choose. When Arjuna's narrow self-interest is abandoned there remains just one will: the will for realization of his larger source Self. It is here that the wills of Krishna and Arjuna unite in one seamless awareness of the original source self. This is the highest path. It is the path of love and light.

As a warrior-in-the-making, Arjuna finally wins the fight with himself. His self-conquest is complete. When his fighting with himself is over, the fighter evolves as the warrior. From the follower's perspective, this transcendence involves the discipline of restraint of the will of the individual, and receptivity to the will of the universal cosmic order. The higher powers of human nature are coded in the cosmic order. This order is accessible to all warriors who follow the discipline of self-restraint and the freedom of higher self-exploration. Paradoxically,

$$\text{Evolutionary order} = \text{Discipline} + \text{Freedom}$$

Observe how a tree grows from the soil toward the sky. The soil disciplines the tree and keeps it firmly rooted. The sky sets the tree free to grow in the openness of its vastness. Through this discipline and freedom the tree becomes part of a larger evolutionary cycle of Nature. It is here that all the paths of knowledge, action, and devotion—the head, hands, and the heart—gather together in self-surrender to the cosmic will.

The narrator of the ensuing war, Sanjaya, who has just described the conversation between Krishna and Arjuna to the blind king, Dhritarashtra, now has the timeless truth for us: When the wisdom of Krishna combines with the skill and attitude of Arjuna—wealth, victory, and right order are bound to follow.

# CONCLUSION

# ARJUNA'S AWAKENING

## Practical Wisdom for Timeless Leaders

The *Bhagavad Gita* is a timeless text for leaders that was composed by the philosopher-poet, Veda Vyasa, in the context of the battle of Mahabharata. This text is a battlefield sermon delivered by Krishna to Arjuna. The battle was a fight between the families of two cousins, Arjuna and Duryadhona, representing the Pandavas and the Kauravas. Arjuna is the chief archer and the leader of the Pandavas, and Krishna is his best friend, charioteer, and his battle-field coach. The context in which the 18 sutras of the *Gita* play out is not unfamiliar to the leaders of today. The psychological context of the *Gita* is the breakdown in performance of the leader, Arjuna. Arjuna suffers symptoms that are all-too-familiar to us in our own stressful times: grief, loss of meaning, and inability to carry the burden of mounting performance pressures.

The genius of poet Veda Vyasa crafts a poetic treatise on leadership in the middle of a historic battle that took place in Kurukshetra, which still exists in North India. In ancient India, history was not written down, as it is today. History was reported orally, as with the commentator on the ensuing battle of Mahabharata, whose name is Sanjaya. Sanjaya is a character in the story who reports on the battle like a modern-day television commentator. Yet the story of the historical battle of Kurukshetra goes beyond mere factual reporting of events.

Vyasa brilliantly transports us from the specific context of the battle—bound to a certain time and place—to those timeless human problems to which leaders throughout the ages have sought solutions. When Arjuna quizzes his coach, Krishna, on the origin of the wisdom that was being delivered on the battlefield, Krishna replies that he had delivered the same message many thousands of years ago and to many leaders before Arjuna. "How is that?" asks the surprised Arjuna. "You, Krishna, were not even born when this wisdom was supposed to have been delivered by you." Krishna replies that this wisdom does not originate in the physical structure of a human being but in the timeless consciousness that transcends the birth and death of the human form. Krishna says, "I will be born again and again when this wisdom is lost in the tide of times. When injustice and untruth overshadow order and harmony in the universe I will incarnate in the human form many times to deliver this timeless wisdom."

Krishna represents the advent of wisdom when it is sorely needed. But what makes his wisdom so essential today? What practical aspects of wisdom are relevant to our times? Let us explore the following elements of the wisdom of Krishna as they lend themselves to the world of leadership practice.

## QUIET LEADERSHIP: THE PRACTICE OF HANDLING INFORMATION OVERLOAD

Visualize a conversation on performance enhancement as a battle is about to begin. The two people involved are lead-archer Arjuna and his wise mentor and charioteer, Krishna.

Arjuna's head is overloaded with information that he finds difficult to digest. His senses are assaulted by the sound and fury of the battle. His mind is unruly; his emotions are out of control. Now, let us see Arjuna's plight in our own context.

A leader in today's workplace often finds himself stuck on the information superhighway and unable to make headway. The Internet, which was supposed to liberate us from the limits of space and time, now binds us in cyberspace and sleepless time. The eyes of a typical professional move from one screen to another in rapid succession. He can focus on each screen for barely 10 seconds on average. The battle of bleeding-edge communication technologies for his mind is incessant and insistent. How does the brain of a leader cope with the kind of neural noise that it must withstand? Krishna calls for a reflection-break for Arjuna in the middle of the hectic activity as a practical method for handling information overload. In Sutra 6, he counsels Arjuna on the art and practice of meditation so that Arjuna can effectively master his own mind.

The busy mind, Krishna argues, is a mob of unprocessed thoughts and emotions. The only way to deal effectively with this mob is to create distance between the mob and the observer, who can now see the mob without being part of it. This observer within the leader is like the screen on which a filmed drama is projected. There are a lot of sensations, a lot of twists and turns of information and emotion in this drama—a riot of sound and colour—yet the drama of the film does not affect the screen. Krishna's solution to information overload is the rigorous discipline of observing one's thoughts and emotions as though they were no more than images on a screen. A leader can gain the composure and quietude of the observer by constant practice and dispassion. This is the practice of watching one's thoughts, as and when they arise, and dispassion toward emotions whether of joy or sorrow. Krishna is urging the leaders of our time to evolve a reflective consciousness rather than a reactive mind. In short, his message for our time is: *Once in a while, be quiet!*

## LEADERS MUST FIRST SOLVE THEIR MOST PERSISTENT PROBLEM

Krishna advises Arjuna that his most persistent problem is a preoccupied mind. What makes leaders deficient in their occupation is their preoccupation. It is their constant preoccupation with their problems that prevents them from truly understanding that the most significant part of the problem is not *out there* in the world but *in here*, in their preoccupation. It is not that there are no problems in the environment; there *are* problems. But when leaders add to these problems the burden of their own fear and anxiety regarding them, the problems become even more complicated. Most of the international border disputes between war-ravaged nations, a depressed economic climate, the environmental gloom, predatory businesses depleting Earth's resources at an alarming rate—all of these originate in the problem-infested mind.

Krishna urges Arjuna to observe the very nature and composition of his mind. The mind that is constantly in motion with its ceaseless preoccupations cannot see the truth of a situation. This mind is like a turbulent lake that cannot reflect the image of the Moon without distortion. This blind dynamism of the mind is preoccupied with thoughts of fear, anxiety, guilt, and shame. This only perpetuates the darkness in our world, for thoughts sooner or later become things. Thought is the internal motion of the mind while action is the external motion. Thought force becomes organizational and societal forces. The truth of the matter is buried underneath the turbulence of thought. A system, a procedure, or another person out there cannot liberate the person from the problem—only the perception of truth will. Only the truth liberates.

Timeless leaders cannot solve their most persistent problems by thinking through them. They cannot think of the problem simply because their thinking itself *is* the problem! Krishna's message to leaders is very clear: Your most persistent problem is *the mind that clings to fear and anxiety* as a way of justifying its existence. *This* mind will lose its identity if its most persistent problems are solved. Therefore, this mind does not want to let go of its fear and anxiety. Krishna is drawing the leader's attention not to the anatomy of the problem but to the contours of the mind that has a vested interest in keeping the problem in its place. The only way to solve this problem is to face the truth: No problem exists without the mind's active participation. Therefore, Krishna urges leaders to walk the path of truth. They can do so only when they have an open and unoccupied mind—a mind that does not live in prejudices and dogmas. Such a mind is uncluttered by reactions and memories of the past. This pure mind reflects the light of truth like a mirror. The mirror truthfully reflects whatever stands before it whether it is beauty or ugliness, fear, joy, or anxiety. Yet the mirror itself does not react or become conditioned by what it reflects. This mirror-like awareness will solve the world's most persistent problems at their source.

## WISDOM IN TIMES OF UNCERTAINTY: LEADERS DEAL WITH DISCONTINUITIES IN LIFE AND WORK

The wisdom of the *Gita* teaches us how to deliver results in uncertain times. A core capability that all leaders of all times must possess is the ability to lead change. Change brings with it the experience of uncertainty. In times of change, business-as-usual no longer works. The global financial downturn, the rising of unemployment in the United States, the economic crisis in Europe, the natural disasters in Japan, new technology and automation making old business processes obsolete, the fall of autocratic regimes in the Middle East, the gradual rise of Asia and Africa as economic powers—all of these and more have challenged the status quo like never before.

In times of uncertainty our old mental models, based on our past history and past experiences, no longer hold good. When the rate of change outside our mental worlds become greater than the change within us, we feel like victims of circumstance. This is what causes Arjuna's despair. He feels that the stable order and norms in his society will be destabilized if he decides to go to battle. Krishna transports Arjuna's attention from the battle outside to the battle within his mind. He explains that in the evolving life of a human society conflict is inevitable. The source of this conflict is not the society outside but the distortions arising inside our own minds. The mind is linear and clings to the comfort zones of the past. Reality outside the grasp of the mind is ever-changing and ever-dynamic. By clinging to what is familiar, Arjuna's mind has distorted reality. Without understanding and transforming his mind, the disorder in his outside world cannot be set right.

Krishna challenges Arjuna's utopian thinking and his shallow alibis that tempt him to shy away from performance. Leaders must first understand the nature of a mind that is stuck in a certain mood or mode, like an airplane on autopilot. Just as turbulent weather challenges a pilot's navigational skills, the uncertainties of life and work require the higher-order navigational capability that comes from pure awareness of the Self rather than from the conditioned models of the mind. Krishna urges Arjuna to challenge and change his mental models, which no longer deliver. Today's leaders must remain relevant and useful to the world they choose to serve in. To do that, they need to deal with discontinuities and question their own mental models.

## LEADERS TRIUMPH BY MERGING THEIR INDIVIDUAL WILL WITH LIFE'S PURPOSE

Krishna asks Arjuna in Sutra 18 to go beyond wishful leadership to wilful leadership. *Wishful* leadership is a passing fancy or a weak impulse in the mind that does not translate into action. *Wilfulness* signals a leader's bias for action. A leader is never more decisive than when he decides to act. Arjuna must give up wishing, for he cannot both wish and will. The two mental forces are utterly incompatible. The first inhibits action; the second inspires action. Krishna finally succeeds in awakening in Arjuna the will to pick up his bow and arrow, which he had dropped in despair. He is now set for the battle. From being wishfully disengaged, Arjuna is now wilfully reengaged with the work at hand.

The human will is a subtle and powerful force. Leaders have to learn to harness this willpower in a way that makes this will an indomitable force. There is a paradox of willpower: Willpower diminishes in intensity when it is employed to achieve a personal goal. On the contrary, the same willpower is magnified manifold when it is invested in achieving a purpose beyond one's narrow interest. If a room is locked up and all doors and windows and all apertures are closed, the air inside the room will stagnate and become poisonous. However, when the doors and windows are open the stale air will be freely exchanged for the fresh air from outside. Willpower stagnates and becomes poisonous within the psychological boundaries created by personal ambition. The same willpower sustains greater life when it merges with the purpose of the larger environment.

The most successful and enduring business organizations of the past century, those that have outperformed the market many times over, have been the ones with purposive leadership. Jim Collins, the renowned leadership researcher, points out that the leaders of such organizations live the paradox of personal humility and fierce professional will, with which they pursue the larger organization's purpose. In the *Bhagavad Gita*, Krishna asks Arjuna to apply the same principle in the business of life. Arjuna is advised by Krishna to surrender his personal will to the larger purpose, for which his life should be lived. In his heart, Arjuna surrenders and becomes humbly receptive to the quiet wisdom of Krishna, even while his hands rise in fierce resolve to resume the battle.

Arjuna's purpose is not to annihilate his adversaries. His purpose is not even to fight a battle, although this is what he eventually does. His purpose is to establish *dharma* or righteousness by restoring to its rightful claimant the kingdom of Hastinapur, which the Kauravas had wrongfully captured. Inspired Arjuna realizes that his business is with the work-at-hand and not with the results, which will be shaped anyway by the greater purpose of the Universal Will. Like stagnant air in a closed room experiences the rush of a breeze when the windows and doors are opened, Arjuna experiences an inrush of energy from the inexhaustible source and reservoir of the larger purpose. Thus empowered, and as the battle of Kurukshetra comes to a close, Arjuna and the Pandavas finally outperform the mighty Kauravas. The kingdom of Hastinapur is won back and righteous *dharma* is established.

# REFERENCES

Axelrod, Alan. 2010. *Gandhi CEO*. New York: Sterling.

Barks, Coleman. 1995. *The Essential Rumi*. New York: HarperCollins.

Besant, Annie. 2009. *Thought Power*. Chennai: Theosophical Publishing.

Chatterjee, Debashis. 1998. *Leading Consciously*. Woburn, MA: Butterworth-Heinemann.

Chatterjee, Debashis. 2008. *Leadership Sutras*. New Delhi: Elsevier.

Chidbhavananda, Swami. 2000. *The Bhagavad Gita*. Tiruchirappalli: Sri Ramakrishna Tapovanam.

Chinmayananda, Swami. 2007. *Holy Gita Ready Reference*. New Delhi: Chinmay International Foundation, Ernakulum.

Chinmaya International Foundation. 2011. *Bhagavad Gita Course*. Chinmaya International Foundation, Ernakulum.

Chopra, Deepak. 1993. *Ageless Body, Timeless Mind*. New York: Crown Publishing House.

Dando-Collins, Stephen. 2000. *The Penguin Book of Business Wisdom*. New Delhi: Penguin Books.

Dayananda, Swami. 2001. *The Teaching of the Bhagavad Gita*. New Delhi: Vision Books.

de Mello, Anthony. 1998. *One Minute Nonsense*. Anand: Gujarat Sahitya Prakash.

Fenster, Julie M. 2000. *In the Words of Great Business Leaders*. New York: John Wiley & Sons.

Gandhi, Mohandas K. 1996. *Mind of Mahatma Gandhi*, edited by R.K. Prabhu and U.R. Rao. Ahmedabad: Navajian Publishing.

George, William. 2002. *Authentic Leadership*. San Francisco: Jossey-Bass.

Handa, Sunil. 2006. *Stories from Here and There*. Ahmedabad: Eklavya Education Foundation.

Hawley, Jack. 2001. *The Bhagavad Gita*. Madras: East West Books.

Judge, William Q. 1999. *Notes on the Bhagavad Gita*. Mumbai: Theosophical Company.

Kellerman, Barbara. 2004. *Bad Leadership*. Boston, MA: Harvard Business School Publishing.

Kotter, John P. 1997. *Matsushita Leadership*. New York: The Free Press.

Kumaraswamy, Anand. 2006. *Gandhi on Personal Leadership*. Mumbai: Jaico Publishing.

Lal, P. 2005. *The Bhagavad Gita*. New Delhi: Roli Books.

Mashelkar, Raghunath. 2010. *Timeless Inspirator: Reliving Gandhi*. Pune: Sakal Publications.

Mehta, Rohit. 1995. *From Mind to Super-Mind*. New Delhi: Motilal Banarsidass.

Mehta, Rohit. 1955. *Seek Out the Way*. Chennai: Theosophical Publishing House.

Meligi, Moneim El-. 2006. *Leading Starts in the Mind*. Singapore: World Scientific Publishing.

Osho. 2006. *Krishna: The Man and His Philosophy*. Mumbai: Jaico Publishing.

Parrinder, Geoffrey. 1999. *The Bhagavad Gita*. New Delhi: Research Press.

Prem, Sri Krishna. 2008. *The Yoga of the Bhagavad Gita*. New York: Morning Light Press.

Radhakrishnan, S. 2006. *The Bhagavadgita*. New Delhi: HarperCollins.

Ramakrishna, Shri. 1998. *The Gospel of Shri Ramakrishna*. Kolkata: Ramakrishna Ashram.

Rama, Swami. 2004. *Perennial Psychology of the Bhagavad Gita*. Honesdale, PA: Himalayan Institute Press.

Row, Jaya. 2006. *Profile of the Perfect Person*. Mumbai: Jaico Publishing.

Schweig, Graham M. 2007. *Bhagavad Gita*. New York: HarperCollins.

Sidle, C. Clint. 2005. *The Leadership Wheel*. New York: Palgrave Macmillan.

Swami, Shri Purohit. 2005. *Bhagavad Gita*. Mumbai: Jaico Publishing.

Thakar, Vimala. 2005. *Insights into the Bhagavad Gita*. New Delhi: Motilal Banarsidass.

Tutu, Desmond. 2000. "Let South Africa Show the World How to Forgive," *Knowledge of Reality* 19.

Vivekananda, Swami. 1992. *The Complete Works of Swami Vivekananda*. Calcutta: Advaita Ashrama.

Wilhelm, Richard, and Oswald, H.G., trans., *Lao Tzu*. New York: Penguin Books.

Yogananda, Sri Sri Paramahansa. 2005. *The Bhagavad Gita*. Mumbai: Jaico Publishing.

Yogananda, Sri Paramahasa. 2005. *Man's Eternal Quest*. Kolkata: Yogoda Satsanga Society of India.

# ABOUT THE AUTHOR

**Professor Debashis Chatterjee** has taught leadership classes at Harvard University and at the Indian Institutes of Management (IIM), Calcutta, Lucknow, and Kozhikode, for nearly two decades. He has been awarded the prestigious Fulbright Fellowship twice for predoctoral and postdoctoral work at the John F. Kennedy School of Government at Harvard. His published work includes six books, such as *Leading Consciously* (Foreword by Peter M. Senge) and *Break Free* (Penguin), that have been translated into several international languages. He has trained more than 10,000 managers globally in Fortune 100 corporations and has served as leadership coach to political leaders and CEOs of major Indian organizations. He has served as Dean of an international business school in Singapore. A pioneer in the field of Asian models in leadership, Professor Chatterjee is currently Director of the IIM, Kozhikode. He also serves as an independent director on the boards of several multinational and Indian companies. He can be reached at successsutras@gmail.com and on the Web at www.debchat.com.

# INDEX

Information overload, practice of
    handling, 212–213
Insight, 127–130
    darshan (world view), 127–128
    timeless dance of life, 128
    sight and insight, 128–130
    seeing through the mind's eye,
      126–128
Inspiration, 22–26
Integral vision, 125–134. *See also* Vision
Integration, 81–91, 152–153
    dharma and, 85–87
    diversity and, 84–85
    egocentric leadership, failure of,
      87–88
    eye of wisdom for, 152–153
    freedom of "I am," 81–91
    head and heart, 152–153
    human spirit, elements of, 82–83
    human suffering, liberation from,
      89–91
    journey from ignorance to wisdom,
      82–83
    spirit-centered leadership, 87–88
    team spirit, 83
    unity and, 81
Integrity, 85
Intellect, 29–31
Invincibility, 12–13, 17–31
    conquest of the binary mind, 12–13
    discontinuity and, 12–13
    wisdom and, 17–31
Invisibility, 151–153, 165–173
    detachment and, 168–169
    integration of head and heart,
      151–153
    knowledge and, 167–169
    leader role to make visible, 169–171
    pattern recognition and, 152
    perishable and imperishable forms of
      nature, 172–173
    seeing with the eye of wisdom,
      151–153
    self, 169–171
    source of, 165–173

    supreme self, search for using,
      172–173
    tree of life and, 165–169

**K**
Karma yoga, 33–45
Kartavya bhavana (renouncing
    personal aggrandizement), 203
Knower of the field, 145, 149–151
    changes in field and, 148–149
    detachment and, 168–169
    eye of wisdom and, 146–149
    fields of, 146–149
    invisible source and, 167–169
    tree of life and, 167–169
    true, 147–148
Ksanti (renouncing emotional
    outbursts), 202–203

**L**
Leadership, 1–16, 17–31, 47–57, 69–79,
    81–91, 110–112, 113–123,
    158–161, 175–183, 185–193,
    195–209. *See also* Timeless
    leadership
    awareness, 2–3
    being and becoming, 110–112
    choices, 3–8
    consciousness and, 113–123
    crossroads of, 175–183
    ego and, 8–12, 15–16
    egocentric, failure of, 87–88
    faith and, 185–193
    forces of nature harnessed by, 158–161
    herd instinct, 4
    inspiration, 22–26
    integration and, 81–91
    intellect, 29–31
    invincibility and, 12–13
    law of giving, 110–112
    mastery of the mind, 73–77
    meditation and, 69–79
    mental model for concentration,
      18–20
    motivation, 22–23